Before CRISIS Hits

Building a Strategic Crisis Plan

Larry L. Smith
Dan P. Millar

Community College Press®
a division of the American Association of Community Colleges
Washington, D.C.

The American Association of Community Colleges (AACC) is the primary advocacy organization for the nation's community colleges. The association represents 1,100 two-year, associate
degree–granting institutions and more than 10 million students. AACC promotes community
colleges through six strategic action areas: national and international recognition and advocacy,
learning and accountability, leadership development, economic and workforce development,
connectedness across AACC membership, and international and intercultural education.
Information about AACC and community colleges may be found at www.aacc.nche.edu.

Community College Press
American Association of Community Colleges
One Dupont Circle, NW
Suite 410
Washington, DC 20036

Printed in the United States of America.

ISBN 0-87117-345-X

Contents

1 What Is a Crisis and Why Should I Care?

As a college administrator, you will never face a crisis that someone else has not already experienced.

And you will never encounter a crisis you cannot manage if you keep your head, surround yourself with good people, gather and confirm the facts, identify the audiences or stakeholders you need to reach, and have a crisis operations and communications plan ready to activate at a moment's notice.

In this opening chapter, we provide definitions and examples of crises that have devastated community colleges and other institutions of higher education. In subsequent chapters, we offer proven techniques and strategies—supported by examples—that will help you manage the crises you are likely to face sometime in your career.

What Is a Crisis?

Endowments are not growing. There is more competition for faculty and staff. Test scores are slipping, and the debate team is off to a losing season. Those problems are just that: problems, a challenge, but not a crisis.

For the discussion that follows, we define a *crisis* as an event or issue that triggers negative stakeholder reactions that affect the college's reputation, financial strength, and ability to carry out its mission.

Based on years of research and experience, the Institute for Crisis Management (ICM) has determined that there are four types of crises in higher education: *sudden, bizarre, perceptual,* and *smoldering.*

Hair-Raising Headlines!

These actual newspaper headlines and leads are just a drop-in-the-bucket sample of the kinds of crises that strike community colleges and other institutions of higher learning every year.

- A California Community College student was taken into custody and 14,000 De Anza College students and staff were evacuated.

- Jefferson (Kentucky) Community College was threatened with loss of accreditation.

- A Hoosier college student got drunk, fell down, and bumped his head. His drinking buddies carried him to his room and put him to bed to sleep it off. Instead, his brain started swelling, and he died in his bed several days later.

- The former Dean of Student Development at Central Methodist College in Fayette, MO, faces charges of starting two fires at the school.

- In fact, there are an estimated 1,700 fires on U.S. college campuses annually, according to the Federal Emergency Management Agency.

- A college president was accused of falsifying his credentials, and a professor from his own staff created a Web site calling the new president a fraud. The Board of Trustees decided to stand behind their choice but did not explain why. The administration set out to fire the tenured professor.

- Critics say Oakland Community College wasted thousands.

- Lawsuits increase as campus attacks do; colleges scramble to improve security.

- Community Colleges of Spokane criticized for hiring decision; African American groups says SCC chief should have gotten job.

The Sudden Crisis

The sudden crisis is the type most people think about: fires, explosions, natural disasters, violence on campus, and, now, terrorist attacks. These kinds of crises usually make a splash in the headlines and on local television news; most organizations rise to the occasion or at the least muddle their way through them.

A sudden crisis occurs without warning and generates news coverage that can adversely affect:

- your faculty, staff, students, alumni, suppliers, and other publics

- your offices, classrooms, infrastructure, or other assets

- your budget, fundraising, endowment, and investments

- your reputation—and ultimately your community college's ability to recruit staff and students and maintain alumni support

Many colleges have operational crisis plans that cover sudden crises such as building fires or laboratory explosions. These institutions stage mock crises or other kinds of tests to gauge the worth of these plans.

The Bizarre Crisis

Unlike the sudden crisis, you cannot plan for a bizarre crisis. For instance, at an Indiana college, a student was crushed between two elevators in a campus building. The investigation uncovered the sport of "elevator surfing," in which a student climbs through the emergency door in the ceiling of an elevator car and rides up and down the elevator shaft on top of the car.

The Perceptual Crisis

Like the bizarre crisis, the perceptual crisis is hard to anticipate in your crisis operations or communications planning.

In the corporate world, Proctor & Gamble (P & G) coped with a perceptual crisis for decades. Every few years, someone would reignite the rumor that P & G's stars-and-moons corporate logo was a sign of the devil and conclude that P & G was run by devil worshipers. This usually led to calls for a boycott of P & G products.

Higher education is not exempt from perceptual crises. For example, there are small institutions of high

The Many Faces of Sudden Crises

Sudden crises can take diverse forms. Here are some examples:

- A campus-related accident results in significant property damage.

- A member of your campus community or a prominent visitor dies or suffers a serious illness or injury.

- Your community college is the source of a discharge of dangerous chemicals or other environmentally hazardous materials.

- Accidents at your community college cause the disruption of computer, telephone, or utility service in surrounding areas.

- Your community college suffers a significant reduction in electrical power or other services essential to its functioning.

- A natural disaster disrupts operations and endangers the lives of students, faculty, and staff.

- An unexpected job action or labor stoppage disrupts campus functions.

- Workplace violence occurs that involves faculty, staff, students, or visitors.

quality that constantly fight the misperception that because they are small they cannot offer a good education.

The Smoldering Crisis

The most likely type of crisis to challenge you as chief administrator of a community college is the smoldering crisis.

A smoldering crisis starts out small and internal, usually between two people, and simmers or smolders just out of public view for days, weeks, or even longer. It does not become a real crisis until one or more of your stakeholder groups find out about it.

Sudden or Smoldering: It Can Go Either Way

Crisis situations can be either sudden or smoldering, depending on the amount of advance notice you receive and the chain of events in the crisis. Examples include:

- academic scandal
- judicial action against the institution
- anonymous accusation
- misuse of research
- competitive misinformation
- threat from a disgruntled employee
- computer tampering
- whistle-blower threat or action
- damaging rumor
- neighbor's crisis
- discrimination accusation
- licensing dispute
- disclosure of confidential information
- lawsuit that is likely to become publicized
- equipment, product, or service sabotage
- false accusation
- employee death or serious injury

- leaking of private information about a student
- employee involvement in a scandal
- student safety issue
- extortion threat
- grand jury indictment
- contacts by an investigative reporter
- grassroots demonstration
- adverse government actions
- indictment of an employee
- union organizing
- disruption of academic schedule by severe weather
- sexual harassment allegation
- criticism by an interest group
- strike, job action, or other work stoppage
- terrorist threat or action
- illegal or unethical behavior by an employee

It could be sexual harassment or some form of discrimination. It could be an academic scandal: grade fixing or bad research. It could be recruiting violations in the athletic department. Embezzlement and mismanagement are other examples of smoldering crises.

Consequences of Crises

Whether you are dealing with a sudden, bizarre, perceptual, or smoldering crisis, there will be consequences.

The greatest concern is often about dollars. If your community college is the focus of negative news, there is always the risk of financial loss. Alumni contributions are delayed, reduced, or halted. Major benefactors have second thoughts. Enrollment falls, and fees generated by tuition take a nosedive.

Concurrent with this decline in revenue will be the unexpected expenses of paying for the crisis. Every crisis has a cost, and rare is the institution that budgets for it. For example, if a tornado takes the roof off the administration building and flattens the main classroom building, insurance will pay for part of the repair and replacement, but probably not all of it.

If a group of students files a lawsuit against the community college, claiming a professor was allowed to harass them, or if a group of minority faculty members files a lawsuit accusing the college of discrimination in its promotion and pay policies, the legal fees will soar. If the institution loses, a settlement will cost thousands, if not millions, of dollars. Those legal costs and settlement fees must come from somewhere—and that somewhere is the bottom line.

Suppose your legal counsel is sitting in your office and says you have to find half a million dollars to cover legal fees and a settlement the judge has recommended. Before you turn the page, stop and think back over the current budget. Where can you cut half a million dollars? What program can you eliminate or scale back? How many staff and faculty members can you lay off and still meet your students' needs?

Crises make and break careers. To be successful, top administrators must have the support of alumni, board of trustees, faculty, staff, and students. A poorly managed crisis leads to mistrust of the administration and ultimately to a change in leadership.

The reputation of the college and its president suffers when a crisis strikes. The longer the crisis goes on, the more damage it does, and the harder it is to get under control and overcome.

And then there is the specter of legal action. All the while, the president, top executive staff, board of trustees, and faculty leaders are distracted from their goal of operating a first-class institution and providing their students a quality education.

Albright College in Pennsylvania is experiencing a smoldering crisis that could have been prevented from becoming a significant public crisis; even after the crisis went from smoldering to a full-blown crisis, the damage could have been minimized. Instead, it went from a one- or two-week story to a two-year story. Faculty members have resigned. Fundraising has been hurt by as much as 15 percent, according to a whistle-blower.

The reputation of the college has been questioned by the *Chronicle of Higher Education*. The college's competitive position has been undermined. Competition for funding, students, faculty, and staff suffers when an organization's reputation is challenged in this way. So do staff and student morale.

Albright's crisis began smoldering in January 1999, when a search committee began screening candidates for the president's job. One of the finalists was Colonel Henry Zimon, an army officer ready to make a career change. In February 1999 the search committee recommended Colonel Zimon, and within days a faculty member began a crusade to unmask the new president as a fraud. The professor's line-by-line check of Zimon's résumé raised questions about the new president's honesty and integrity. Through the spring and summer, the controversy smoldered on the campus and in faculty discussions, and the board of trustees became aware of the brewing crisis.

Albright College had several opportunities to prevent the smoldering crisis from becoming a nightmare and to minimize the damage that had already been inflicted. Within weeks of his appointment faculty queries were directed to the trustees, and later in the spring, numerous requests were made for Mr. Zimon and the board to reconcile discrepancies in the new president's résumé. But those opportunities slipped by, and in October 1999 the *Chronicle of Higher Education* took the story beyond the Reading, Pennsylvania, campus and presented it to a nationwide audience.

Throughout the winter of 1999-2000, the board of trustees, the whistle-blower, and the faculty executive committee battled back and forth; meanwhile, the *Chronicle of Higher Education* published three more stories about the Albright College controversy. In August 2001, President Zimon took part in what was billed as a communitywide meeting at which he responded to many of the accusations about discrepancies in his résumé. He did not, however, satisfy the faculty member who was his principal accuser.

By the end of the year, the board reaffirmed President Zimon as their man, but Professor Achal Mehra claimed victory when Albright College ended efforts to fire him later in 2001.

The only consequence of a crisis that has not yet befallen Albright College, or at least been threatened, is government or regulatory intervention. However, Albright College could still face questions from its accreditation organization.

The whistle-blower was more adept at using modern communications tools than the college administration. He created a Web site in which he chronicled his battle against the president and his supporters on the board of trustees. The Web site added to the embarrassment of the entire campus community and alumni and had the effect of undermining the reputation of the school and department where the whistle-blower was employed.

Some Harsh Realities of Academic Crises

Most crises can be predicted and prevented, and those that cannot be avoided can be minimized. Chapter 2 details the history of crises in higher education during the 1990s. One of the significant facts that arises from that review is that three-quarters of college crises start out as smoldering issues.

If a smoldering crisis is recognized for what it is, usually it can be prevented from becoming a full-blown "public" crisis. When it cannot be avoided altogether, there is usually enough time to develop a strategy for minimizing the damage and speeding the recovery process.

The main difference between a sudden crisis and a smoldering crisis is the amount of time you have to prepare to react. A sudden crisis requires an immediate response to secure the safety of people and property, and reporters frequently find out about the crisis before the college president does.

When a smoldering crisis is spotted, you may have hours, days, or weeks to decide how best to manage the problem, to anticipate when and how it will become public, to prepare a response and designate a spokesperson, and to develop a plan to speed recovery.

A serious organizational problem does not become a "crisis" until one or more of your publics finds out. The longer a crisis goes on, the more damage it does to reputation, fundraising, enrollment, and public support.

And management denial is often the biggest obstacle to effective crisis management.

Smart, experienced, educated community college presidents can look straight at a pending disaster and convince themselves that nothing like that could ever happen to an organization they lead. There is another group of equally bright men and women who can convince themselves that if they ignore the problem, it will go away. It rarely does!

One of the most dangerous misperceptions of crisis management is the belief that the college should focus solely on the court of law, when in fact it should be focused on the court of public opinion *and* the court of law.

It will take the courts 18 to 36 months to decide if you took the right action or made the correct decision. It will take the court of public opinion 18 hours or less to make up its collective mind about how you managed things.

For decades, lawyers have been advising clients to keep their mouths shut and not say anything that might jeopardize a future ruling. Unfortunately, in today's much smaller world, word spreads rapidly and rumors take over when facts are not available. If your community college is in trouble or perceived to be in trouble, there will be plenty of sources willing to talk, speculate, and frame your story from their point of view. Faculty, staff, students, and alumni will talk among themselves. They will talk about either the facts as you have presented them or the rumors that fill the void you have created. What do you want them to repeat?

This is not to suggest that you tell everything you know and say whatever you want. Your message needs to be carefully crafted, with each word carefully chosen, and legal counsel is an important part of that process. But to say nothing speaks volumes.

Think about any company, college, or organization that has been in crisis in recent times. If, after a reasonable amount of time, you did not see a spokesperson, what was the first thing that came to your mind? They have something to cover up.

A quick and simple statement is all it takes to get started, acknowledging to the media and public that you are aware of their interest and intend to be as straightforward as possible. "I don't know" is a good answer in the first hours of a crisis; "I don't know but we're going to find out" is a better answer.

Sometimes, for security or investigative reasons, you may be limited in what you can say. It is still important to acknowledge to your various audiences that you are aware of their questions and explain why you cannot say more immediately. Honesty and forthrightness will buy you time. Dodging, ducking, and deceiving will make the whole crisis immeasurably worse.

The object of the process is to get to the end of the litigation, win, and still have a viable institution without losing the support of faculty, staff, students, alumni, and the community.

In the past, when an organization stonewalled and ignored the court of public opinion, it could get three years down the road and finally receive a favorable court ruling, only to discover that there was really nothing to celebrate. While public opinion was being ignored, the staff would have drifted away, students would have gone elsewhere, and contributors would have had enough doubts about the administration to withhold financial support. In such a situation, any legal victory would ring hollow.

The President's Role in Crisis Management

The community college president has responsibilities that no one else can assume and often attempts to assume responsibilities that should be delegated to others. Unless the administrative staff and the college itself are very small, the president should not be a member of the crisis management team. (The makeup of the crisis team is addressed in chapter 3; the specific duties of the president are outlined there.)

However, the chief executive officer (CEO) of the college will ultimately be responsible for the outcome of the crisis management effort and at the same time continue to be responsible for the ongoing operation of the institution. One of the mistakes CEOs frequently make is to activate the crisis team without making it clear that its top priority is to manage the crisis, not its members' day-to-day duties. Those day-to-day responsibilities must be delegated so that they do not distract the crisis team members from the immediate task of getting the crisis under control.

Another mistake top executives often make is to ignore advice to "settle" an issue, while insisting on standing on "principle." Sometimes good administrative practice requires resolving the problem or smoldering crisis in a reasonable, legal, and ethical way and getting on with the business of running the institution.

There are scores of examples of organizations where ego or principle dictated the decision-making process. And managing any crisis is time consuming, often expensive, and distracting. When you are distracted by the crisis, you are not concentrating on the job for which you were hired. And while you are distracted, other problems tend to develop and smolder and then, because no one is paying attention, blow up into another crisis, compounding the first.

2 Sources of Crisis in Higher Education

Explosions, fires, and chemical spills probably will not be your undoing as a community college president, but crises caused by discrimination, mismanagement, and sexual harassment might. We do not mean to denigrate the importance of the typical crisis because fires, explosions, and chemical spills can injure and kill. However, we do mean to indicate that they occur less frequently than other kinds of crises—ones that may seem less frightening but can undermine your credibility and authority, as well as the integrity of your institution.

In this chapter, we briefly discuss the nature of organizational crises in general, and those crises most commonly experienced by postsecondary institutions in specific. Our purpose in this analysis is to demonstrate your need, as a community college president, to prepare for those crises most likely to occur at your institution.

Database of News Stories

The Institute for Crisis Management maintains a database of almost 80,000 news stories collected since 1990. Gathered from more than 1,500 newspapers, business magazines, wire services, and newsletters worldwide, these stories all focus on organizational crises. There is information on all types of organizations in the database, not just commercial enterprises.

The stories are catalogued into 16 categories of crises experienced by organizations. Data can be retrieved by:

- nature of the crisis

- industry

- organization

- year (by quarters)

- geographic location

- sources quoted within the news story

Duplicate stories are deleted as part of the coding process, so the database contains only original stories representing crises since 1990.

Changing Nature of Organizational Crises during the 1990s

Table 2.1 identifies 16 categories of crises most frequently experienced by organizations in the news stories in the Institute for Crisis Management database. The table shows that the total number of stories in the categories of

Table 2.1 Crisis Categories Compared— All Organizations*		
	1990	2000
Catastrophes (natural disasters)	5.5	5.0
Casualty accidents	4.8	4.9
Class-action lawsuits	2.2	28.4
Consumer activism	2.8	1.6
Product defects and recalls	5.4	16.7
Discrimination	3.3	3.5
Environmental damages	7.8	1.9
Executive dismissal	1.3	0.8
Financial damages	4.2	4.4
Hostile takeovers	2.6	0.5
Labor disputes	10.3	11.3
Mismanagement	24.1	6.3
Sexual harassment	0.4	0.5
Whistle blowing	1.1	0.7
White-collar crime	20.4	9.3
Workplace violence	3.8	4.4

* Expressed as percentages of the year's crises.

labor disputes, class-action lawsuits, and product defects and recalls went up from 1990 to 2000, while the number in the categories mismanagement, environmental damages, and white-collar crime went down. Figure 2.1 focuses on the changing nature of higher education crises during the decade.

Because people typically think of fires, explosions, and toxic spills when thinking about crises, they might believe that heavy manufacturing and petrochemical industries might be the most crisis-prone. Our analysis suggests otherwise, as reported in Table 2.2.

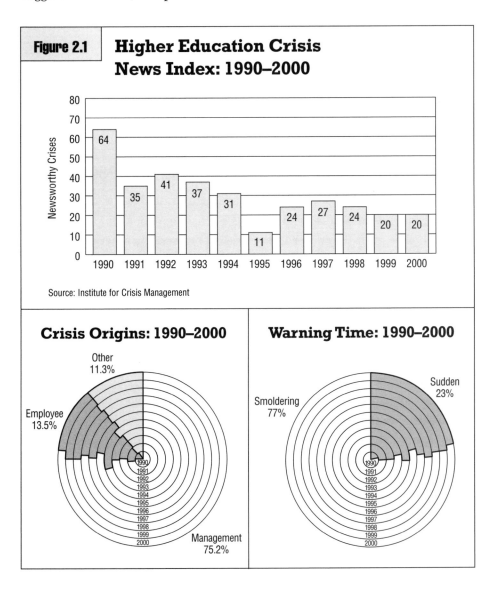

Figure 2.1 | **Higher Education Crisis News Index: 1990–2000**

Source: Institute for Crisis Management

Crisis Origins: 1990–2000

Other 11.3%
Employee 13.5%
Management 75.2%

Warning Time: 1990–2000

Sudden 23%
Smoldering 77%

Table 2.2	**Most Crisis-Prone Industries, 1990s***

1. Banking and related activity	6. Aerospace
2. Stock and bond brokering	7. Telecommunications
3. Insurance	8. Air transportation
4. Motor vehicles manufacturing	9. Computer software
5. Oil and gas extraction	10. Pharmaceuticals

*Measured by percentage of incidents recorded in the ICM database.

Heavy manufacturers do appear on the list, but not because of an abundance of fires and explosions. Rather, they appear because of labor disputes, product defects and recalls, and class-action lawsuits. Fortunately, higher education does not appear on the list.

Nature of Higher Education Crises during the 1990s

Nonappearance on the list of crisis-prone industries does not translate to "no crises." What we do find is that the kinds of crises experienced by institutions of higher education differ from those experienced by other organizations. Table 2.3 shows that your community college is more likely to experience a crisis resulting from discrimination, mismanagement, or white-collar crime than one growing out of class-action lawsuits, environmental damages, or natural disasters.

Some of these crisis categories either increased or decreased steadily during the past decade. For example, the percentage of catastrophes progressively declined while that of casualty accidents slowly increased. The proportion of sexual harassment crises steadily increased throughout the decade, perhaps as a result of a heightened awareness leading to a greater willingness to report an incident. Crises related to financial damages, mostly awards from lawsuits or government fines, consistently increased throughout the period.

However, crises related to workplace violence, labor disputes, and discrimination all became markedly more common toward the end of the 1990s, as shown in Figures 2.2 and 2.3. The same graphic displays crisis concentrations over the 1990-2000 period, information that is presented in list form in Table 2.3.

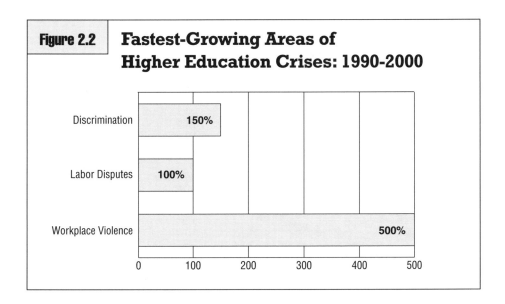

Figure 2.2 | **Fastest-Growing Areas of Higher Education Crises: 1990-2000**

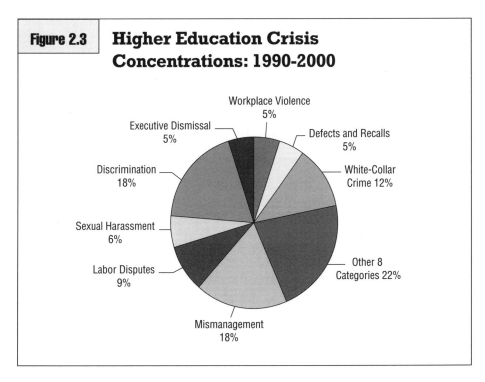

Figure 2.3 | **Higher Education Crisis Concentrations: 1990-2000**

Crisis Categories Compared—
Higher Education*

	1990	2000
Catastrophes (natural disasters)	6.3	4.1
Casualty accidents	1.6	4.1
Class-action lawsuits	0.0**	1.2
Consumer activism	12.5	3.3
Defects and recalls	1.6	5.3
Discrimination	17.2	18.9
Environmental damages	3.1	2.1
Executive dismissal	3.1	4.7
Financial damages	0.0	4.4
Hostile takeovers	0.0	0.0
Labor disputes	7.8	8.6
Mismanagement	40.6	17.8
Sexual harassment	0.0	6.2
Whistle blowing	0.0	3.0
White-collar crime	4.7	11.5
Workplace violence	1.6	4.7

* Expressed as a percentage of the year's crises.
** A percentage of 0.0 does not mean that no incidents of this crisis occurred
but that the number reported was less than 0.05 percent.

While community colleges differ from other types of higher education institutions, many of the crises experienced by the other types may be experienced by community colleges, for example, problems with parking lot security. A forest of blue lights has grown during the past 10 years, alerting students, faculty, and staff to the location of emergency phones and video cameras on campus parking lots.

So what were the sources of crisis during the 1990s? Organized on the basis of the 16 crisis categories tracked in our database, the lists on the following page identify examples of the kinds of crises experienced by institutions of higher education.

These lists demonstrate the range of what can go wrong at your community college. Their length also underscores a point we made in chapter 1: There are no new crises. If it has happened to someone else, it can happen to you. Your best defense? Preparation.

Crisis Can Visit Your Campus in Many Forms: A Sampling

Catastrophes

- An earthquake is blamed for a decline in admissions applications.
- A flood destroys library materials.
- A hurricane closes an off-campus laboratory.
- A tornado damages college buildings.
- Lightning strikes destroy campus computer laboratories.

Casualty accidents

- A student injured in a chemistry laboratory blast sues the college and a teacher.
- Buildings at California colleges and universities that are not earthquake-proof are considered "potential deathtraps."
- The Federal Aviation Administration boosts oversight of aviation programs because of an increase in student pilot accidents and deaths.
- Students are killed in cars and vans en route to or while attending college-sponsored events such as athletic activities, debate and forensic events, and music contests.

Class-action lawsuits

- A college is sued for unpaid staff overtime.

Consumer activism

- Students stage protests regarding on-campus speakers, admission policies, racial and sexual hiring, quality of education, budget cuts, tuition increases, and World Trade Organization and World Bank policies.
- Students stage a hunger strike over a lack of funding for a Chicano studies program.

Defects and recalls

- Lax security leads to increases in campus crime.
- The presence of polychlorinated biphenyls (PCBs) or asbestos requires colleges to close and demolish campus buildings.
- Flaws in standardized tests are deemed unfair to minority and disadvantaged students.
- Programs fail to meet accreditation standards.

Discrimination

- Georgia schools are told to halt policies that "aid minorities."
- Academic institutions extend—or do not extend—benefits to gay and lesbian couples.
- Gays, lesbians, African Americans, Latinos, older employees, or other groups experience potentially discriminatory termination of employment.
- A state technical college is cited for racial discrimination.
- A professor sues over alleged sexual discrimination.
- Students sue over alleged religious discrimination.
- Faculty sue over denial of tenure on alleged racial or sexual grounds.

Executive dismissal

- A department chair is ousted for "racially disturbing remarks."
- A dean quits in a dispute with the board of trustees over a lack of faculty and staff raises.
- State regents oust board members at a New York State school for "poor oversight" of administration.
- An ousted chief executive officer sues a college for millions of dollars.
- A college board of trustees ousts a chief executive officer for "poor communication."
- A dean is fired because of an "appalling lack of collegiality," according to an accrediting body.

continued on pg. 18

continued from pg. 17

Financial damages

- A fired vendor receives $6 million in a suit against a college.
- Two fired by a college are awarded damages totaling $195,000.

Labor disputes

- A strike by employees closes a college dining hall.
- College secretaries and clerical workers strike.
- Faculty and staff strike for "raises."
- College staff strike for a better health plan.
- College janitors strike to get recognition of their union.

Mismanagement

- A college is found guilty of false advertising of its programs and is fined by the Federal Trade Commission.
- A Louisiana politician's relatives and friends attend a college tuition-free.
- A college is accused of nepotism in its hiring practices.
- A college participates in illegal "fixing of aid limits" for students using federal funds.
- A college's improper billing to the federal government is revealed by an audit.
- Open-meeting laws are violated by faculty governance councils, administration committees, and boards of trustees.
- College officials make improper contributions to political parties.
- Lax campus security results in rapes and subsequent lawsuits under the Violence Against Women Act.

Sexual harassment

- Colleges try to hide "violent sexual harassment."
- Date and acquaintance rape becomes a source of campus problems.
- Faculty require students or staff to engage in sexual activities in exchange for good grades or job security.

- A college president makes obscene telephone calls to women from his office telephone.

Whistle-blowing

- An auditor blows the whistle on improper use of royalties.
- A secretary blows the whistle on improper counselor behavior in clinical services.

White-collar crime

- Faculty, staff, and administrators submit fraudulent résumés.
- A college chief executive officer diverts donations to a personal account.
- Employees steal supplies, materials, equipment, and money.
- Faculty make and use illegal copies of licensed software.
- Colleges count illegal aliens as residents to receive state reimbursement dollars.
- Administrators submit fraudulent insurance claims.
- Faculty sell drugs to students.
- Faculty use their offices for paid professional activity.
- Students, faculty, and administrators gamble on athletic contests.
- Faculty illegally duplicate and distribute copyrighted materials.

Workplace violence

- Campus shootings occur: student to student, student to faculty, significant other to faculty or staff.
- The Violent Crime Control Act forces colleges to open their records on campus crime.
- A prospective student is charged with sexual battery while visiting a college campus.
- A student is raped while on a college-authorized trip to a foreign country.

3 Building the Crisis Management Team

A large part of preparation means eliminating the conditions that can cause a crisis: poorly lit parking lots, absent or incomprehensible policies, poorly maintained storage facilities holding chemicals or other potentially toxic materials, untrained faculty and staff, poor oversight of financial units. Prepare to respond promptly and properly to those crises that cannot be prevented—storms, power outages, computer failures, accidents.

Your community college's crisis preparation process includes building a crisis management plan and assembling a team of people to implement it. This chapter describes the selection process for a crisis team, the responsibilities of that team before and during a crisis, and the role of the president when a crisis strikes.

The Crisis Response Team: Duties and Chain of Command

You should clearly identify the members of the communications team and their responsibilities, as well as their backups, in the crisis communications plan. You should keep the team leadership relatively small—three or four persons—with a designated backup person for each team leader. You should designate one person, preferably a trained communications professional, as communications coordinator, with at least one backup deputy.

The communications coordinator serves as the principle communications adviser to the crisis manager. The crisis manager is the person responsible for directing your community college's overall response to the crisis. So that you might make the most of your executive staff's range of subject-area expertise, the identity of the crisis manager should depend on the nature of the crisis. Figure 3.1 suggests a structure for the crisis management organization.

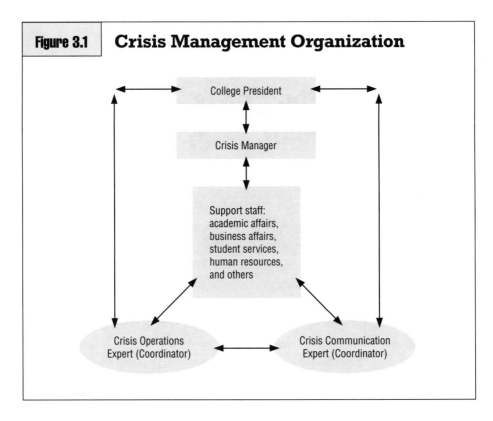

Figure 3.1 | **Crisis Management Organization**

Depending on the nature of the crisis, the team may include representatives of academic affairs, public relations, business affairs, facilities management, human resources, legal counsel, minority resources, student services, information systems, government relations, development, institutional research, and safety and security. But all college officials prepared to serve on a crisis team might not be called upon at one time. Only those members with skills and knowledge necessary to manage a specific crisis should be pressed into action.

For example, if a domestic dispute that led to a shooting occurred on campus, the crisis team might include representatives from student services, safety and security, government affairs, and the executive office (the executive vice president or provost).

The team member from student services has oversight of student records and supervises student counselors and possibly a counseling clinic. The safety and security representative brings investigative abilities, knowledge of police procedures, experience managing crime records and safety and security equipment, familiarity with campus safety and security issues, and a working relationship with community law enforcement agencies.

The government affairs team member should also have a relationship with local law enforcement personnel, as well as with local, state, and federal elected and appointed officials. A familiarity with local medical professionals and facilities is also helpful.

The representative from the executive office is familiar with the thinking and expectations of the president and other members of senior management and possesses training and experience in speaking for the community college to key publics such as students, employees, faculty, staff, and the news media. If the crisis grows because a faculty member was part of the love triangle that sparked the domestic quarrel, the team might add a representative from academic affairs.

Should your faculty be governed by a collective bargaining agreement and a faculty member is involved, your team might have to include a representative from the union. In the case of criminal activity, your legal counsel is a necessary addition to the team.

However, two constants on the team should be a representative of the executive office and a member of the communications staff. The executive representative is key because the executive offices have ultimate responsibility for the college and (presumably) authority to mobilize its resources to respond. Their representative on the crisis management team need not necessarily be the president.

Likewise, the communications staff member is important because regardless of the nature of the crisis, your key stakeholders will have to be addressed. While the executive might be the primary spokesperson, the communications staff will gather information, write media releases, prepare briefings, develop materials for the media, oversee the placement of information on the college's Web site, and send blast e-mail to employees. In other words, the communications staff will keep the crisis management team and the executive branch of the college informed about the various publics' reactions to the crisis and keep these publics informed about what the college is doing to deal with the tragedy.

The members of the crisis team and their responsibilities, as well as their backups, should be clearly identified in the plan.

The crisis team should know from the plan who is responsible for handling the crisis response operation and who is required to review and approve internal and external communications. The people responsible for approving crisis communications should understand the importance of speedy and careful review and prompt approval to facilitate timely communications to all audiences.

Several of the community college crisis plans reviewed for this book include only operational personnel. While those plans might effectively prepare the college to react to a toxic chemical spill involving campus maintenance personnel, they will not necessarily provide guidance on how the college will communicate to students, parents, faculty, neighbors, regulatory agencies, and staff affected by the spill.

Classifying the Seriousness of a Crisis

A classification system allows an organization to assign different levels of response, depending on the severity of the crisis. For example, a sudden crisis can have as many as four levels, starting with the least damaging.

A "Level 1" crisis would be an event that requires incumbent staff to respond to something out of the ordinary. It can be handled by the people on duty and will not draw any outside attention from the media or other audiences. A Level 1 crisis usually does not require an immediate response from the community college's public relations office or crisis team, although both should be notified as a matter of normal reporting.

A Level 1 crisis might involve an attempted break-in to the college's computer system. No one but the computer department manager and campus security will need to know, but at some point the administration, including the communications director, should be notified.

A Level 2 event usually requires that some staff be called in early or held over to assist, but the event is not likely to draw attention from the public.

A Level 3 or 4 crisis requires outside assistance, such as police, fire, or other emergency services, and will draw attention from neighbors, staff, students, and the media. Immediate notification of the crisis team is mandatory.

Usually the difference between a Level 3 and 4 is the degree of impact and how much attention will be focused on the crisis.

The team should regularly update the president on its management of the crisis. The team might meet in the president's conference room to facilitate the communication between it and the CEO of the college. The president should not be a member of the team.

Notifying the Crisis Response Team

You should compile a thorough directory of the full crisis response team, including backups. This directory should include each team member's office phone, home phone, fax, mobile phone, and pager numbers, as well as home and office e-mail addresses. If the team member has a second home or vacation residence, be sure to include the contact number there as well. Update the directory regularly, at least once each semester or academic session. Personnel turnover, internal promotions, and job reassignments can render a plan virtually useless if it does not reflect who is currently responsible for each crisis team task and all the up-to-date access numbers for each team member.

The crisis team should maintain close contact with anyone in the college community with firsthand knowledge of the specific crisis. These people can be valuable sources of details and in many cases can provide guidance on how to communicate with various audiences. For example, there has been an incident in a chemistry lab. A chemistry professor or chair of the department could be invaluable in managing the crisis and framing public comments and responses.

Line and Staff Responsibilities

Other employees with communications skills can be given specific assignments that will help ease the pressure on the crisis communications team during the initial stages of a sudden crisis. For instance, they can answer the deluge of calls from the community and the news media that is sure to occur, logging the names and telephone numbers of callers so that the crisis team can determine who should receive a follow-up response.

Whenever a statement has been released to the public, they also can be instructed to read the copy in response to questions: for example, a typical news release or statement usually begins with words such as "We can confirm at this time...." All statements and news releases should be based on confirmed information. No one should ever speculate in public comments.

Other staff, human resources personnel for instance, can compile background information on employees who might be affected by or involved in the crisis. Likewise, student affairs personnel can quickly provide information on any student affected by the crisis.

If you have someone who prepares radio and television releases, your audio/visual staff can record radio and television newscasts and provide summaries of the substance of the crisis coverage to the communications center. Those summaries should include the station's call letters and frequency, date and time of the newscast, the name of the reporter, and a brief summary of the story, highlighting any errors or surprises.

Your food service personnel, or servers from your contracted food service, may be assigned to line up food and drink to support the efforts of the crisis response team and, if you establish a media center, the journalists who gather there.

Training the Crisis Team

No team should be expected to manage a crisis without some practice. Tabletop exercises, simulations, and full-fledged drills can prepare your team to react promptly and properly. A member of your staff can plan and facilitate an exercise or simulation, or you can also hire consultants to do the training. (We provide further information about training in chapter 5.)

More about the President's Role

Ultimately, the community college president makes the decisions that set the policy and procedures for dealing with the crisis. But that does not mean the president needs to be constantly involved in the strategic discussions of the crisis team.

No one person or office can carry the load of communicating throughout the duration of a sudden crisis. As the crisis progresses, various people play crucial roles in reaching important audiences. Some crisis writers recommend that you select a single spokesperson, usually the president, to be your primary contact with the media for the duration of the event. We do not concur with that recommendation for three reasons.

First, community college presidents need to manage the organization through the crisis. Guiding the organization through the chaos to a return to relatively normal activity should be the president's primary goal. Second, if the president serves as the primary media spokesperson and misspeaks, no one else can correct the error without significant embarrassment to the president, the college, and the board of trustees. Third, the cause of the crisis may be the president, in which case having selected the person in that position as the principle spokesperson becomes problematic. Internal chaos may result as other senior executives jostle to become—or avoid becoming—the spokesperson.

The president does play an important communications role during the crisis. It is appropriate for the president to speak to:

- students and employees and their families, particularly if the crisis involves casualties

- key government officials such as the local government's chief executive, legislators, and key regulatory officials

- key stakeholders, including opinion leaders and major donors and vendors

- other educational, religious, civic, and government leaders

In performing its role, senior management will reaffirm communications policy (it should be established during creation of the organization's crisis plan) for the duration of the crisis. The president is the appropriate person to express the sorrow and sympathy of the institution to victims and their families. This expression of condolences can occur as part of the overview of the crisis situation. That overview need not be the first statement made by your community college. You may have already made the initial comments disclosing whatever confirmed information is available in the early stages of the crisis. However, not long into the crisis the president ought to make an appearance with remarks addressed to the key audiences.

One last but very important role played by the president is that of final arbiter for the crisis team. Should the team become divided over a strategic or tactical decision, the president can break the stalemate.

The success of a spokesperson—whether the president or some other official—depends on how good a job the communications staff does at gathering information and preparing the spokesperson. The media and community relations staff coordinate the gathering and dissemination of information as well as the preparation of key personnel, while monitoring the media's coverage of the crisis. Many community colleges do not dedicate full-time staff to communications. If that is the case for your institution, assign that responsibility to someone you trust who has a network of sources both within and outside the college and a working knowledge of the information needs of the news media. Then, make sure that person gets the required training to hone his or her communications skills. Should a crisis arise, divert this ad hoc communications official from his or her normal responsibilities and, once the crisis has been resolved, be sure to recognize this individual's unique contribution in a tangible way—perhaps a one-time stipend, special achievement award, or other form of monetary compensation.

The president's role in a crisis can be boiled down to five tasks:

- continue to guide the college
- confirm or modify the strategic decisions of the crisis response team
- express sympathy, or other appropriate responses, of the institution
- be prepared take over as spokesperson if designated spokesperson makes a mistake
- break any deadlocks occurring within the crisis team

The selection and training of the crisis communications team and its members' integration with the operations team are only one part of your preparation for a crisis. Another part is the creation of a crisis plan or plans. That task is the focus of the next two chapters.

4 Building the Crisis Communications Plan

Managing a crisis without a communications plan is like showing up for the big game without knowing who the opponent is or having a game plan. The game starts without you while you call a team meeting to decide who will guard whom, who will lead the team, and who will take the shots.

By the time you get organized, the other team has scored 25 points, and before you can even think about winning, you have to try to overcome the advantage you gave away while trying to figure out what to do first.

You would fire a coach who approached any game that way. But that is exactly what you are doing if you run a community college and do not have a crisis plan ready to use at a moment's notice.

In this chapter, we tell the story of a community college that had a crisis plan and used it. We also outline ways you can build your own crisis communications plan.

One Morning in Cupertino, California...

At 8:30 a.m., January 30, 2001, in Cupertino, California, the Santa Clara County Sheriff's Office called Martha Kanter, president of De Anza Community College, and reported finding 60 bombs and booby traps and an arsenal of weapons in the home of a 19-year-old De Anza student. The Sheriff's Office had also found a map of the campus showing where the student intended to place the explosives.

President Kanter promptly activated the campus disaster plan, taking on the role of emergency operations director. The vice president for finance and college services took charge of a campuswide evacuation, while the chief of campus safety became the incident commander. The incident commander began working with the Santa Clara County sheriff and agents of the Federal Bureau of Investigation and the Bureau of Alcohol, Tobacco, and Firearms. Within two hours of the call from the Sheriff's Office, 14,000 staff, faculty, and students had evacuated the campus, and law enforcement officials had begun a systematic search for bombs and booby traps in and around 65 buildings on the college's 110 acres.

To complicate the evacuation, De Anza had about 2,000 students whose mobility was impaired in some way by a physical disability. However, the college kept records of where each of those students was at any given hour, and individuals were assigned to go to them and assist them in case an evacuation was ordered. That part of the evacuation plan worked well.

By 3 p.m., the authorities had declared the campus safe, and by 6 p.m. the okay was given to resume classes. Several thousand students were on their way to night classes before the all clear was given, and the crisis team had to divert that traffic away from the campus, all the while working on the plan to resume a normal class schedule the next morning.

De Anza Community College had a crisis response plan and a team that had trained together. A command post went into operation almost immediately after the sheriff's call the morning of January 30, and the members of the response team were soon at work, executing their respective responsibilities. As with all good plans, each team member had a trained backup. Normally at De Anza, the director of communications would have been in charge of coordinating the media center and the emergency operations center, but the director was off campus at a meeting that morning. However, the media coordinator stepped up to work with the local and national news media representatives who descended upon the scene.

A Good Crisis Management Plan Is Actually Three Plans

Much of the success of De Anza Community College's crisis management plan can be attributed to the fact that it was actually three plans: an *emergency response plan* to guide college officials through the first nerve-wracking hours; a *crisis communications plan*, which included guidance on how and what to communicate to students, faculty, and staff, and the community at large; and a *recovery plan*, which ensured that while the campus was being searched for explosives, planning was already underway for how and when to resume classes once the all-clear was sounded.

Thanks to the involvement of risk managers and insurance companies, most organizations have at least a basic plan for emergency response operations. Recovery planning is the logical extension of this operations plan and lays out the steps and process by which an institution gets back to normal.

This chapter focuses on how to integrate a communications element into your community college's crisis response plan.

Components of a Crisis Communications Plan

A crisis communications plan has three components:

- the philosophy and policy behind the plan
- the heart and soul of the plan: how to manage specific crises
- worksheets and checklists

The first few pages of the crisis communications plan should include a letter from the president explaining why the crisis plan is important and making it clear that the president is depending on the crisis team members and will support them in the difficult task they have agreed to do.

This philosophy and policy section also defines the types of crises covered in the plan and identifies the crisis team members and their responsibilities, as well as their respective backups. This section should also include a directory of telephone numbers and e-mail addresses for all members of the team (including backups).

The second section of the crisis communications plan is the heart of the plan: the communications strategies that coincide, step by step, with the action steps in the existing operations response plan.

The third section consists of the worksheets and checklists that help the crisis team members carry out the preplanned steps in the second part.

But First, the Vulnerability Study

Before you can write the crisis communications plan, you must determine the kinds of crises your institution might experience and then develop the plan accordingly. Some people call this process an audit. We call it a *vulnerability study.*

The first step in a vulnerability study is to take a look at the kinds of crises that have struck other institutions of higher education. Since there are no new crises, someone, somewhere, has already experienced what you may face someday. A search of education journals and the mass media will reveal examples of the kinds of crises that get attention beyond a college campus. (We also provide some examples in chapter 1.) The second step is to prepare a questionnaire and identify one to two dozen administrators, faculty, students, and alumni and survey them on their perceptions about crises that could befall your community college. The survey respondents should include a representative cross-section of administrators, faculty, staff, students, and alumni.

The first question to ask is: When you go home at the end of the day, what do you worry about most that could go wrong and damage the reputation and financial stability of our community college? This general question can lead to the more pointed questions that appear on the following page.

Once the vulnerability study is complete and you compile the responses, the list of potential crises will probably include many, even most, of these:

- a terrorist attack on campus

- a student with a gun

- a classroom fire

- an explosion in a classroom laboratory

- an academic scandal (cheating, altered test scores, plagiarism)

- budget deficits, fundraising problems, or embezzlement

- charges of sexual, age, or gender discrimination

- lawsuits, in particular class-action lawsuits

- fatalities or injuries resulting from binge drinking on campus

Potential Crises Survey

Your general question about potential crises can serve as a lead-in to more pointed questions such as these:

1. What kind of management notification system do we have in place if a crisis occurs outside our hours of operation? How long would it take to reach everyone on the Crisis Management Team if we had a crisis at 3:00 p.m. on a Saturday? What is our campus emergency response plan like? When was it last updated? Has it ever been used or tested to see if it works? How well does it tie in with the response plans of our other facilities?

2. What internal problems or other vulnerabilities do we have that could be damaging to our community college if they became public knowledge? What would be the public reaction if one of them were disclosed by a disgruntled employee, or in a lawsuit, government investigation, or investigative news report? How would we explain or justify the situation so it would have minimum academic and financial impact on our community college? What is being done to minimize the chances of that problem occurring?

3. Who would be our spokesperson in a crisis situation? Who would be the alternate if the spokesperson were not available or not appropriate for that kind of crisis situation? How good would the spokesperson be at handling tough questions from reporters? How much confidence do we have that the spokesperson would be credible and convincing? How would disclosures be handled at one of our facilities if it experienced a crisis? Who would be the designated spokesperson?

4. How much information would we give out if we had a crisis? Who would decide what to say? What would be the approval process? How long would it take?

5. How would we go about contacting the college administration and employees to ensure that they would hear from us before learning about the crisis from the news media? How about our students, alumni, and other key audiences?

6. Can you think of any crisis situations similar organizations experienced in the past year that became public? How well would our community college have handled those crises? How much management time did that crisis take up? How much has it cost the affected institution so far in expenses and lost funding? How likely does it seem to you that the affected institution will face lawsuits or government investigations? How long do you think it will be before that institution puts the problem behind it? How would we have done if it had happened to us instead of them? What can be learned from their experiences? Have we made any changes in the way we do business as a result of what happened to them?

- questions about the safety of female students on campus

- demonstrations on campus by animal rights, environmental, or pro-life groups

- right-wing protests against expressions of academic or artistic freedom

- staff labor disputes

- whistle-blower charges

- weather-related class disruptions

- computer hacker attacks on grade databases or other sources of confidential student information

One crisis that usually does not come up in a vulnerability study but that nonetheless warrants consideration when you are developing a crisis communications plan is the death or incapacity of a top administrator, particularly the president, the vice president of academic affairs, or the provost. Another crisis communications plan category that should be considered is "a seriously negative news story."

It will not be necessary to write 18 separate crisis categories. Several of the potential crises on the list above can be managed with the same approach and similar plans.

Based on the sample vulnerability study, the crisis plan could have the following basic plan elements:

- Aggression against the college

- Fires, explosions, and natural disasters

- Academic, athletic, or administrative scandal

- Legal actions

- Student affairs crises

- Campus protests and demonstrations

- Computer failures and attacks

- Labor trouble

- Death or incapacity of a senior administrator

- A seriously negative news story

Each crisis category should look similar to this example:

CRISIS: Aggression on Campus and Workplace Violence

Crisis Team Leader:_____

Office: _____Fax: _____

Home: _____Pager: _____

Mobile: _____

Deputy Crisis Team Leader:_____

Office: _____Fax: _____

Home: _____Pager: _____

Mobile: _____

In an era of terrorism and random violence, an act of aggression against your college or one of its facilities cannot be ruled out. Possibilities include workplace violence, armed assault or robbery, bombings or bomb threats, kidnapping or hostage taking, exposure to hazardous or toxic substances, and extortion. Should one of these or a similar aggressive acts occur, the safety of faculty, staff, students as well as the general public is paramount.

Depending on the nature of the crisis, the families of victims and/ or other faculty, staff and students could be in danger. In that case, the administration will work with authorities to make appropriate security arrangements.

Communications Priorities in the Event of Workplace Violence or Other Aggressive Acts on Campus

If the aggressive act is an armed robbery, hostage taking, hijacking, bombings or bomb threats, workplace violence, or kidnapping, communications activities should be coordinated with the police or other authorities to ensure that nothing is done that might further endanger the lives of those affected.

You should focus on these six audiences following workplace violence or other aggressive acts that occur on campus:

- faculty and staff
- families of the victims

- students

- vendors and contractors

- alumni

- the local community

In any instance of aggression, the communications priority is to reassure employees and students and keep the families of victims fully and continually informed. The names of victims should be withheld until their families are notified. The police normally make the initial notification. The initial statement to all audiences should come as soon as possible and from the community college president, if possible. It should include two messages: (1) an expression of sympathy, from the president personally and from the college collectively, for victims and family members; and (2) a pledge of cooperation with the investigating authorities.

Communicating with Employees and Students

Staff and students must be reassured that activity will get back to normal as soon as possible and that their work or study areas will be safe. The college should immediately arrange for counseling to be available to staff and students. Counseling services may already be available through the college's employee assistance plan or even through the faculty that teach that specialty. This should include establishment of a hot line that is staffed at least 12 hours a day. Staff and students will need someone to talk to and will have a variety of questions. Not all questions can be answered immediately, but the hot-line worker can take the question, get answers, and call back with the college's response. Like all members of the crisis team and support staff, telephone hot-line operators should be identified and provided training *before* a crisis strikes. Mid-level faculty and staff are the best source for this task.

Staff and students will want to know when they can go back to the classrooms, and they will want information about their injured friends or co-workers or funeral arrangements for victims.

Communicating with Victims' Families

If your community college is struck by an act of aggression, it is a near certainty that the news media will learn about it almost immediately after it happens. You can more effectively manage the course of events—and, even more important, mitigate the pain of victims' families—if you can ascertain the names of victims so that the police can inform the families before that information is made public. The crisis team, in cooperation with the college administration, is responsible for communicating with victims' families.

Once the police have made the initial contact with victims' families, a designated campus representative should contact them in person immediately to provide any further information known to the college administration. If the families are believed to be in danger, make sure that law enforcement officials give them instructions about what to do until security arrangements go into effect. The campus representative should advise the families that any inquiries from the news media should be referred to the crisis coordinator at your community college. The families should refer calls from unknown persons to the police.

In case of death, serious injury, or hostage taking, a campus representative should be dispatched to the victim's home as soon as possible and be prepared to render assistance as required. This representative should:

- Maintain frequent contact with the administrative office in order to keep abreast of developments that should be passed on to the family.

- Learn the names and telephone numbers of the family doctor, clergy member, and at least one close friend or relative.

- Shield the family from unwanted telephone calls by having someone screen calls.

- Volunteer to handle any details or problems with which the family might need help. These might include arranging for childcare, having meals brought in, and arranging for transportation and accommodations if the victim has been taken to a location distant from the family's home.

- Offer to assist with funeral arrangements if the victim has died.

- Assure the family that any short-term financial needs will be met by offering a one-time, no-strings attached check for $5,000 and assistance in expediting insurance settlements.

- Remain in touch with the family for as long as necessary to ensure that their immediate emotional needs are met and their questions and concerns are answered in a timely manner.

Communicating with Students and the Community

If the incident takes place on campus, the site will become a crime scene and will be off limits to everyone, including staff and students. If the crime scene is in a dormitory, the college will have to make immediate arrangements to house the displaced students. If it is in a classroom building, laboratory, or library, you will need to post signs redirecting students and staff to alternate facilities.

If a student or employee is killed, members of the community where the incident occurs will pour out their sympathy to the victims, and impromptu memorials will appear in front of the facility. As long as the impromptu memorial does not interfere with classes or other operations, it should be preserved for a reasonable amount of time or until a more permanent memorial is created.

It is appropriate for your community college to work with a neighborhood church or organization to arrange a community memorial service within a day or two of the incident to provide an opportunity for friends and neighbors to participate in the mourning process.

A memorial service should be planned for a few days after the last funeral. It should be limited to staff, students, their families, families of the victims and their friends, and others associated with the college. The president should attend. Media coverage should be limited to pool coverage, and a restricted media area should be designated outside that has visual access but is sufficiently removed from the entryways to the site of the service so that participants can come and go undisturbed.

When your community college reopens, the administration should place an advertisement in the local print media featuring a letter from the college president thanking the community for its sympathy and support.

Communicating with Supporters

Alumni and community relations staff will determine if direct communications with supporters and boosters are necessary to reassure them of the college's ability to recover from the tragedy and meet the unexpected expenses of the event and subsequent settlements and legal actions.

Communicating with the News Media

In a crisis resulting from an aggressive act, the investigating authority is in the best position to know when release of information could jeopardize the investigation or endanger others. For this reason, the investigating authority almost certainly will handle the release of information about the act itself. This does not preclude your college from releasing information about itself— that is, information that ordinarily would be furnished to the media for other purposes.

No information about the incident should be released by the college unless it is specifically cleared with law enforcement officials. Media inquiries about unclear information should be referred to these authorities. Nevertheless, good public relations practice requires that your college cooperate with the news media and assist them as much as possible without impeding the investigation.

To prevent situations in which "no comment" would be the only response, you should draw up a statement, in coordination with the law enforcement authorities handling the investigation, that confirms and summarizes known facts and stresses that the college is cooperating with authorities. Do not release the following information:

- The names of the dead or injured, until it is certain that their families have been notified.

- Details about your college's permanent security system or about any system put in place in response to the crisis. It may be desirable, however, to release a broad outline of the college's security program and policy to show that your institution is security conscious. If this information is released during an actual crisis, the release should be coordinated with the investigating authority.

- Speculation about individuals or groups who might be responsible for the act of aggression, or about possible motives.

- The amount of money taken in a robbery or other details of an incident without approval from investigators.

The crisis team leader should act as liaison between the college and the investigating authority. If possible, a representative of the crisis team should be on the site of the incident at all times to assist with on-site media relations and ensure that law enforcement authorities are receiving the full cooperation of the institution.

Advertising

In coordination with the authorities, the college should consider advertising, posting rewards, or utilizing other forms of communication with the public.

Materials to Guide You through a Crisis

The third part of the crisis communications plan is your compendium of worksheets, checklists, and directories that will guide you through each phase in the management of an on-campus crisis. For a list of these materials, see box at left.

The sudden crisis worksheet and smoldering crisis worksheet are basically lists of questions that include the "who, what, when, where, why, and how" questions whose answers you need to know to manage the crisis and, in particular, your communications about the crisis. The final "letters of agreement" are those documents that should be worked out before a crisis strikes. There should be an agreement spelling out where the crisis team will assemble and work if the main administration building is inaccessible or unusable, as well as an agreement with the telephone service provider to redirect some main telephone lines to an alternate command center.

You should have an agreement in place with a vendor to provide computers, printers, facsimile and photocopying machines, office furniture, and office supplies if the college establishes an alternate command center. Another vendor should be ready to provide extra mobile phones on short notice, and still another should be available to provide food and beverages for an extended operation. There should be an agreement with a counseling service to provide critical incident stress debriefing and grief counseling on short notice. These are just examples of the services that should be lined up in anticipation of future need.

Role of the Internet and Your Intranet Site

Your crisis plan should be printed, and each crisis team member should have three copies—one for the office, one for home, and one to keep in the car. It should also be available on your intranet site.

The crisis team should have access to the crisis operations and communications plans on the college's intranet. All of the worksheets and checklists and other crisis reference materials should be available to download and print from the intranet. A crisis plan is always changing. Team members come and go, telephone numbers change, and additional documents and letters of agreement are added. The print copies might be updated once or twice a year, but the intranet copy of the crisis plan can be changed whenever necessary.

The intranet is a great tool to share information with faculty, staff, students, and other facilities. In Kentucky, there is a network of community colleges and if something happens on one campus, it is usually a good idea to let the other community colleges in the system know, so they are not surprised when a reporter calls and asks, "Could that happen here?"

Because your community college's Web site is another effective tool for communicating with a variety of audiences, including students, alumni, the media, and other interested stakeholders, you should have a "ghost page," ready to activate in case of a crisis. Your computer technical staff can create an area within your Web site that cannot be seen until you declare a crisis and activate the page. Typically, a key word or words (which actually can be more than one word) is created to pop up on the home page and link to the crisis page. The key word should be as neutral as possible. If, for example, you have a fatal fire in the classroom building known as Dickenson Hall, your home page key word linking visitors to the crisis page could simply be *Dickenson Hall.* (We talk more about ghost pages in chapter 6.)

All statements, news releases, and other documents related to the crisis that are made public should be posted on the crisis page immediately, with the latest document appearing first. When reporters begin to call, they should be alerted to the existence of the Web site and "incident" page and instructed to check there for the latest information and to call back if they do not get all the information they need. These crisis Web pages significantly reduce the number of repeat media calls because reporters discover that they can get everything they are going to get, ready to download and print at times convenient for them, without being put on hold or waiting for someone to call them back. If your crisis is a story with appeal beyond the local community, it will accommodate journalists in different time zones and with different news deadlines.

Why Crisis Plans Can Go Wrong

Lack of management interest will doom a crisis plan. The community college president must believe in the planning process and make it clear that the crisis plan is important. Plans that are doomed to fail are often insurance driven, with policies and procedures that are not focused on the major vulnerabilities of the institution.

Another shortcoming of many crisis plans is their orientation toward operational issues, with little or no consideration of communications. Under such plans, the possibility of news coverage is all too often seen as a threat—not a problem or an opportunity. Dealing with the media should almost always be considered an opportunity to tell your story and communicate with key audiences no matter what the circumstances. Just as dealing with the media is an opportunity when you have a positive story to tell, it can be an opportunity when everything is going wrong and you need to explain what you are doing about it.

Poorly developed and poorly written crisis plans become big, dusty, black notebooks on the shelf that give no consideration to the chaos inherent in any crisis.

And, finally, a plan that is never tested or updated is almost guaranteed to fail.

Practice, Practice, Practice

Once the plan is in place, all the crisis team members should come together to practice with the new plan. A tabletop exercise is a good place to make mistakes and learn what is in the plan and how to use it. (See chapter 5 for guidance on practicing implementation of a crisis plan.)

5 Practice with the Plan

Having an untested plan is like having no plan at all, or even worse. In the 1980s, the National Aeronautics and Space Administration (NASA) spent a lot of money to create a first-ever crisis communications plan in case disaster struck a space mission with a human crew. When the plan was finished, a practice was scheduled but later postponed because everyone was too busy.

Before the practice could be rescheduled, the space shuttle *Challenger* was launched and, with the world watching on television, exploded before the eyes of millions of people, including 1,800 reporters and photographers, at Cape Canaveral.

The untested NASA crisis communications plan was put to the test. Unfortunately, NASA security officials had a crisis plan too, and the first task on their checklist was to lock the doors to the control room and not let anyone leave until they had been debriefed. The top NASA public relations managers were in the control room and could not get out to answer reporters' questions for about four hours. The communications delay made the disaster seem even worse.

If the public relations plan had been tested, NASA would have discovered the security lock-down order and made adjustments without the whole world watching.

Some basic truths must be recognized before a crisis plan can be thoroughly tested and implemented. For one thing, crisis timing is invariably awful. Some people think crises only happen during normal work hours. Wrong! A crisis is most likely to occur at 3 p.m. on Friday afternoon, or even worse, at 3 p.m. on Saturday afternoon, when all the key administrators needed to manage the crisis are scattered to the four winds. One is at the lake for the weekend, another is at soccer practice with the children, another is shopping, and still another has taken a weekend trip and no one knows where she is. The longer the crisis goes on, the more damage it does and the harder it is to bring under control. If it takes two or three hours to round up your crisis management team and get them started on their assignments, that is two or three hours deeper in the hole you have to dig out of. And then some of the people you need most cannot help anyway. They are off at a conference half a continent away or on sabbatical.

How do you contact your key administrators? Do you depend on a "telephone calling tree"? Does everyone on the crisis team have a list of everyone else's numbers? And the really important question: Does each crisis team member carry a pager? The president and top administrators and other key staff members should carry a pager and a mobile phone so they can be reached quickly.

If you have a role to play on the crisis team, and it takes two or three hours to reach you, that means you will have that much more to do to catch up. If you had a pager and got notified immediately, you would have a better chance of getting ahead of the problem.

There will still be roadblocks to overcome. Human and hardware communications problems will slow you down. No matter how many telephone lines you have feeding into the campus, there will be more students, reporters, and family members trying to call in than your system can accommodate. The switchboard will crash, and not only will your incoming lines be jammed, you will also have trouble getting outbound phones lines with which to communicate and manage the crisis.

Mobile phones used to be the solution. But now it seems everyone and their children have mobile phones and the cells jam just as quickly as the land lines, making it difficult if not impossible to call for help or discuss options and strategies by phone.

Then there is the inevitable news media pressure and the rumors.

Aftershocks

A crisis is very much like an earthquake. Sometimes the initial quake does a lot of damage, and sometimes it just rattles nerves and the pictures on the wall. However, there will almost always be aftershocks, and sometimes the aftershocks are insignificant and sometimes they do more damage than the initial quake.

Sometimes the aftershocks involve the discovery or disclosure of other problems related to the crisis. Within weeks of the financial collapse of Enron Corporation, it was disclosed that a partner in the accounting firm of Arthur Andersen had shredded important documents the government wanted. Then it was disclosed that a company whistle-blower had alerted the chief executive officer and accountants to questionable accounting practices before the company went bankrupt. About the same time, investigations by federal securities regulators and congressional oversight committees were announced.

Within weeks, hundreds of lawsuits were filed. Each "aftershock" kept the story alive, often pushing it back to the front page or to the lead spot on the network news.

When a mentally unstable student was expelled from the Appalachian School of Law, he came back with a gun and murdered the dean of the law school, a law professor, and a student, and wounded three other people. The Appalachian School of Law is a small "community" institution that opened in the 1990s. It offers a four-year program that was started by the community of Grundy, Virginia, to provide educational opportunities to poor people in the region.

Following the shooting, subsequent stories detailed a number of aftershocks, events, and reactions that added to the damage done by the original incident. There was the disclosure that the alleged shooter was mentally unstable, and the school administration knew it. This was likely to give plaintiffs' lawyers ammunition to use against the school.

The fact that the alleged shooter was a Nigerian immigrant added fuel to the negative public perception of the assailant. There was a news account that police and medical assistance was slow to arrive, and that students took matters into their own hands, transporting the wounded to a hospital in private cars.

Classes were suspended for a week. Additional aftershocks were likely. Enrollment in the tiny rural law school could get even smaller. The school's ability to raise funds could be hurt, and there was the possibility faculty members would decide to teach elsewhere. A new dean had to be hired and a professor replaced. The wives of the two faculty victims were also involved with the school, and they were likely to leave.

Steps to Manage a Crisis

You have a crisis plan and have identified a crisis communications management team. As you develop a training program for your crisis team you must take into account the following:

1. **Develop a response plan that focuses on the likely reactions of key stakeholders and can be implemented quickly.**

   Train your crisis team members to gather as much information as possible and constantly be aware of what you still do not know. Identify the most important stakeholder groups and develop communications strategies for each. The media will be pressuring you, but they are seldom the most important audience.

   Most likely your faculty and staff and students will compete to be the most important stakeholders. Alumni will not be far behind. If you are a state school or supported by an organization or a religious group, then these will be other significant audiences. You will not want to ignore the media, but those other groups are far more important as you plan your communications strategy.

2. **Base everything you say on factual, confirmed information.**

   If you are not sure, do not talk about it. One of the most important rules of dealing with the media is to never speculate. A reporter will ask you what happened. "I don't know" is a good answer in the early hours of a crisis. "I don't know but when we find out we'll share that information with you if it's appropriate" is a better answer. However, when you tell the reporter you do not know what happened, yet, the reporter will come back at you with the question, "What do you think happened?"

   Many people want to be helpful and cooperative, and so the temptation is great to try and help the reporter by speculating about what might have happened. Do not do it! Just because someone at the scene says something, does not necessarily make it true. Confirm the facts before you make a statement.

3. **Notify your administration and communications people as soon as possible.**

   If you have the first indication that a crisis is developing, notify the crisis team leader as soon as possible and start the process of getting the decision makers together to begin trying to gain control of the situation.

4. **Anticipate the reactions of staff, faculty, students, and the news media and be ready to respond.**

Creating a Crisis Management Exercise

Pick a likely scenario and create a series of escalating aftershocks. Set a date the crisis management team can get away from the campus and concentrate on a tabletop exercise.

Start with minimum details of the initial incident, and while the crisis team members are beginning to get organized and to anticipate what is developing, give them a few more details, including a twist they could not have anticipated. Give them 30 minutes to put together their strategy, based on their new crisis plan.

When they are called back to the mock crisis-center conference table, let them begin to outline their strategy, and then interrupt with additional information. Have them incorporate the latest revelations into their tentative strategy even as they are reporting back on what they thought they knew.

Make sure the team identifies and prioritizes the key audiences and determines which ones are advocates, adversaries, or "ambivalent." Then have them prepare key message points for each audience, determine the means of distributing each set of messages, and decide who should be the spokesperson and when each set of messages should be released.

As the day progresses, add additional aftershocks and rate the team on how they cope with each new revelation and complication. To add realism to the exercise, recruit a couple of journalism faculty to play the part of reporters or seek the help of a pair of local reporters, and several times during the day make the crisis team spokesperson go head to head with the "press."

When the exercise is complete, conduct a debriefing exactly as if it had been a real crisis. Determine what worked in the plan and what needs to be improved or adjusted, and then make sure those refinements are incorporated into the plan. Evaluate how individual team members responded and how effective they were in their respective roles.

The crisis team can make or break your institution and your career. This is the time to find out how thorough and flexible the plan is and how effective the team members are.

A Sample Tabletop Exercise

Despite storm warnings reported by radio and television beginning early in the morning, your community college opens for business the Thursday before the start of final exams. The storm hits midmorning. By lunchtime, the wind-driven snow has made driving extremely hazardous. By early afternoon, the governor has closed several highways serving your community, warning people to stay off the roads.

The storm hits with such ferocity that cars in the parking lots are quickly frozen shut by the freezing rain, then buried under heavy snow.

When do you cancel classes? Release faculty and staff? What is your liability if students, faculty, or staff are injured or killed driving home?

Several hundred of your commuter students, using the library and computer labs to finish term papers, are trapped by the governor's road closure announcement. Scores of your faculty and staff cannot get home either.

Do you have responsibility for these people? Where will they sleep? How will you feed them? Will college personnel physically restrain people who want to drive home despite the governor's order?

The storm pounds the college, hitting the student union, in which you have gathered those people trapped by the storm, with particular force. The frozen rain and high wind down power lines, leaving the campus in darkness. The student union, built to allow easy access and egress, has so many doors that the wind blows the cold into the building. Battery-operated radios deliver reports that the storm is not expected to abate until late Friday afternoon.

Friday comes and the governor orders the state police to keep people off the roads until plows have at least cleared major highways and streets and power has been restored. The order makes little difference to the people stranded on your campus because the parking lots cannot be plowed. All available plows, even the private service usually hired by the college, have been conscripted to work the streets so that emergency vehicles can serve the community. By late Friday afternoon, it appears no one will leave the campus until at least Sunday.

How will you care for the trapped people?

This exercise would bring together your crisis team for major storms: academic vice president, student affairs, business affairs, facilities management, and public relations. Support staff might include food service personnel, a counselor, and safety and security personnel. You and the other participants would then implement the crisis plan, including elements related to communication with important publics.

Several such sessions each year will keep the key players in crisis management thinking sharp. They will also help you develop team spirit among key personnel while reducing the probability of errors when a crisis inevitably strikes your community college.

6 Crisis Communication Is Strategic:
Identifying Key Audiences and Preparing to Communicate with Them

- What do you say when several of your music students are killed when their van goes off the highway as they are returning from a statewide contest?

- What do you say when you and other administrators are sued for racial discrimination because a faculty member is denied tenure?

- What do you say when a clerk in the business office is accused of stealing?

- What do you say when the third armed robbery takes place in your student parking lot?

Even in the frenzy of a crisis, what you say and do to key audiences ought to advance specific objectives consistent with the overall goals of your college.

Crisis communication is strategic.

In this chapter we describe a process for communicating with your important stakeholders. The process begins with establishment of a "message platform" that is consistent with the mission of the institution while also relevant to the specific crisis.

Creating a Message Platform

To respond strategically to a crisis, you need to prepare a message platform to complement your operational and recovery crisis plans.

Your message platform can be built long before the hint of any crisis. Some writers use the term *message points.* Some prefer the phrase *message platform* because it conjures the image of an area, a place where you can stand. You cannot stand on "points." The platform is built of simple declarative sentences consistent with the central mission of your community college.

Some Basic Planks in the Platform

While each community college may have a distinct mission, most community college seek to provide:

- a quality education consistent with the demands of a democratic society

- a quality education consistent with the occupational needs of the surrounding community

- opportunities for personal development for their students

- educational, occupational, and personal development to the supporting community at reasonable cost

To those basic planks can be added those required by the particular crisis. For crises that involve investigators or enforcement officers, the plank "working with authorities" can be added. For crises that harm people or animals or the environment, the plank "we are sorry" or "we sympathize" or "we empathize with those injured" can be added. For crises that disrupt the delivery of instruction, the plank "we have arranged for classes to resume" can be included.

Communicating within a crisis should not be reduced to a formula, but much of what you say during a crisis can be prepared before it ever occurs. The message planks or points can be prepared and approved by those in the decision-making process and rehearsed by those most likely to be spokespersons for your institution.

Tell Your Story First

Ideally, you want to utter the words that introduce the story of the crisis. Realistically, that will seldom happen. Reporters and their microwave trucks will beat you to it. Students, faculty, and staff will be guessing about what happened, sharing those speculations in coffee shops, by cellphone, or over the Internet. As more people become aware of the event, rumors will start. People want to know what happened and why. They want to "make sense" of the event.

When a young man approached a female student while she walked across a Florida community college campus, pulled a gun, and shot her in the back of the head (see chapter 7), the more than 20 witnesses wanted to make sense of what they saw. No confrontation occurred. No words were spoken. The woman did not even know the man was behind her. How could this happen? Why did it happen?

In "making sense," the first thought that organizes the random bits of information is the most powerful; it has the greatest effect on how subsequent bits of information will be interpreted. Most of us have played with jigsaw puzzles. What pieces do we try to isolate first? Of course, those that form the edge.

Scores of pieces can be isolated and connected from that one decision. In a similar manner, the first words describing a crisis organize the limited information available and how subsequent information will contribute to the story.

Activate your crisis plan, including your message platform, to begin shaping the story as quickly as possible. If you delay activation, the media—indeed, all your audiences—will begin speculating to make sense. In that speculation they will begin to place blame, particularly if they can demonstrate that you are to blame. Then, they "gotcha!" The sooner you can begin shaping the story, the quicker you can take the "gotcha" out of any media story or the story being told by any audience.

Having a message platform and knowing your key audiences provides a foundation for communicating in the chaos.

Your Community College's Key Audiences

While different crises pique the interest of different publics, most community colleges have some relationship with the following seven audiences:

- students

- faculty

- administrative staff

- parents and significant others

- local, state, and federal government officials

- the supporting community

- the media

Your community college's audiences will want to know the basics of any crisis event: the who, what, why, when, where, and how. Once those questions have been answered, people will want to know what you are doing to end the event, and what, if anything, you had done to prevent it.

You may not need to tell everything, but whatever you say should be verifiable. In the paragraphs that follow, always assume that we assume you will be telling the truth.

Students

Students are the central audience of your community college. Sustaining, even increasing, that audience generates the revenue of the college while fulfilling its core mission. What motivates any one student to attend a community college may vary, but in the aggregate students want:

- a curriculum that will help them become better citizens (although they might not phrase this goal this way)

- academic programs that will make them more employable

- faculty who will teach them to be competent and trustworthy

- sufficient resources to help them succeed in their academic work

- a safe environment in which to achieve their individual goals

Any crisis that undermines the integrity of the curriculum or prevents its delivery, that prohibits students from participating in the curriculum, or that threatens their resources or their physical security will get their attention.

Part of your message should contain statements that assure the students of the college's ability to deliver its programs and that they will be safe while attending. For example, students will want assurance that buildings, equipment, and materials will be available to them following a flood, tornado, hurricane, or major explosion and fire. If the facilities cannot be used, they will want to know what alternative arrangements have been made to provide for continuation of their education. They also will want to know that their safety is not compromised. Many colleges near the Mississippi River and its tributaries had to provide alternative facilities when those rivers overflowed in the mid-1990s.

Reaching the student audience is not easy, particularly under the stress of a crisis. Blast e-mail is one means of reaching this audience. You also can post important messages on the community college Web site assuring students that their education will not be disrupted (assuming it will not), complemented with instructions on what to do, where, and when. Local radio and television provide other vehicles for quickly reaching this audience in a crisis. And, finally, a toll-free hot line that is activated for the crisis can disseminate pre-recorded messages of assurance and instruction. The mechanism needed to set up a toll-free number can be arranged with the local telephone company before the crisis strikes. One call to the telephone company activates the prearranged number.

Faculty

Faculty deliver the courses and programs students want. In a real sense, the faculty assures the integrity of the curricula desired by the students. While individual faculty members—permanent, part-time, or adjunct—may teach at your college for a variety of reasons, generally faculty want:

- a place to practice their profession
- the knowledge that they will be appropriately compensated for giving their expertise to the college
- classrooms with students capable of learning
- sufficient resources to allow them to deliver course content effectively and efficiently

Any crisis that prevents them from teaching, that threatens their compensation, or that undermines their ability to deal with students effectively and efficiently will get their attention.

Part of your message platform should assure faculty that they will be able to continue teaching and be compensated for doing so. When a colleague is let go or denied tenure, the remaining faculty will want assurances that the decision-making process was fair and rational, with the criteria applied in an evenhanded manner. Without such assurances, rumors of discrimination or lack of due process will circulate. Without such assurances, every teacher may feel threatened.

Reaching faculty is easier than reaching students during a crisis. For some smaller colleges, a phone tree may be a quick and efficient means of disseminating information. Assuming the telephones are working at the college, a script of your basic message can be faxed to each department or division with instructions to contact a short list of other personnel. The phone tree must already be in place when the crisis hits if it is to be fast enough to be useful.

The toll-free hot line also is an effective way to communicate with faculty.

Should the crisis hit during off hours for the college, the local radio or television stations may be the quickest means of reaching faculty. More detailed information can be distributed once they return to their offices.

You can also reach faculty through the Internet. Information services personnel can create ghost pages containing message templates for the crises most likely to affect the college. These personnel can activate the ghost page when the crisis hits. A single mouse-click makes information available quickly and thoroughly. As new facts are verified they can be added to the Web site, creating a chronological trail of information about the crisis.

Administrative Staff

Administrative staff support the students and faculty in the delivery of the courses and programs offered by the community college. Their support provides the necessary structure to gather and distribute human and financial resources, to care for the people of the college, and to keep the records needed to prove successful admission into, attendance at, and completion of the college's programs. In general, administrative staff want:

- sufficient direction regarding their responsibilities and some authority to fulfill them

- compensation appropriate to their responsibilities and capabilities

Any crisis that prevents them from carrying out their responsibilities, undermines their authority, or threatens their compensation will catch their attention.

Your message platform should contain assurances that administrative staff will be able to do their jobs even if they will have to do so in unfamiliar places and circumstances. A crisis caused by embezzlement or fraud committed by a staff member sends shudders through other staff, as fears emerge that procedural changes will lead to personnel changes—that people will be replaced and displaced. Staff will seek assurance that their jobs will not be altered drastically or terminated. Without such assurance, the job-related anxiety of the administrative staff will rise, perhaps interfering with the performance of their important functions.

Your message of information and assurance can be carried by the same vehicles used to reach students and faculty: the Internet, hot lines, phone trees, and local radio and television. Some community colleges maintain an intranet. This offers a moderately secure internal environment within which to exchange information. In the embezzlement example, more deliberately paced communication may be appropriate. Speedy communication in this kind of crisis is not as important as in a sudden crisis. Deliberate, careful communication is always best and easier in most smoldering crisis situations. A face-to-face meeting with unit supervisors may be the best method for informing them of the nature of the event and offering assurances.

Parents and Significant Others

Parents and significant others generally, although not universally, provide financial and emotional support to their student. Parents and significant others often provide the financial resources needed by the student to complete the course or program demands of the community college. We lump these two groups together because of the demographics of the community college student body. Many students are much older than traditional undergraduates, already working and, in many cases, raising families. Unlike students, faculty, and staff, parents and significant others are *indirectly* connected to the college. Many college crises that may have an immediate effect upon their student touch them only because of their commitment to their student. Generally, parents and significant others want their student:

- to succeed in the courses and programs of the community college

- to be safe while involved with the college

Any crisis that prevents their student from successfully completing the college's courses and programs or that directly threatens the physical, psychological, or emotional welfare of their student catches the attention of parents and significant others.

A crisis generated by the sexual harassment of students by faculty will cause parents and significant others to question their student's continued attendance at your institution. They will seek assurances that their student is safe from such treatment, that you have rooted out the perpetrators and removed them. Describing faculty governance procedures for the purpose of due process will not assure this group of the safety of their student, although such a message might be reassuring to faculty. Parents and significant others provide a case in which an important message to one public may not be important to another.

The community college Web site, a telephone hot line, and radio and television stories can reach this audience with your message of information and assurance. Because the audience is diverse and in many cases may not live near the college, using regional media may be necessary. In the case of sexual harassment charges against a faculty member, a letter from the president may be the most effective and efficient way to reach parents and significant others.

Local, State, and Federal Government Officials

Education is a regulated industry, with local, state, and federal agencies all playing a role. While they do not directly participate in the central mission of the college—instruction—government officials have direct oversight of many of the college's programs and resources. Generally, government officials want your community college:

- to offer substantive, appealing, cost-effective courses and programs to the community

- to adhere to the laws regulating the institution's performance

Any crisis that reveals that the college is not performing its designated role or exposes the failure of government oversight grabs their attention.

Embezzlement would cause regulatory agents to re-examine their own procedures. The same may be true for sexual harassment. Regulatory officials want assurances that the college is adhering to the policies and procedures prescribed by law. If these are violated, the regulators want assurances that college officials will cooperate with them to resolve and correct the crisis. Failure to pledge cooperation is a red flag that tells the regulatory agent to look closer at the operations of the college.

Elected officials do not respond to the same constituents as regulators. While regulators respond to legislative pressure, elected officials respond to the voting public. Elected officials will be concerned about regulatory failure but equally concerned about crises that threaten the quality of the college's programs. Voters will pressure elected officials to push the college to provide the best education possible at a reasonable cost. Like regulators, elected officials seek assurances that the college will cooperate with government units investigating the crisis.

Elected officials will want assurances that the integrity of the college has not be compromised by the crisis, whatever it may be. In the case of publicly supported or subsidized institutions, those who were elected want to assure those who elected them that taxpayer dollars are well spent.

Telephone calls or personal visits from appropriate college officers may be the best vehicles for communicating with government officials during a crisis. The relatively small size of this audience makes personal contact possible.

A blast e-mail or blast fax, your Web site, and toll-free numbers are also effective vehicles for communicating with government officials.

The Supporting Community

The community provides financial resources that allow your college to operate. Most members of the community have little or no direct connection to the college. However, the community wants an educational institution:

- in which the community can take pride
- that is responsive to the employment needs of both the profit and not-for-profit sectors

Any crisis that threatens the quality of education or prevents the college from providing the community with quality workers directs the attention of the community to your institution. For example, the community may be very attentive when an accrediting body denies accreditation to one of your college's programs.

Because the community is an amorphous audience, reaching it by means of highly targeted vehicles is prohibitively expensive. For this audience, local radio, television, and newspapers may be the most effective methods of communication. Your Web site will be helpful to a plurality of this group. A toll-free telephone number also can be an effective and efficient vehicle. To reach the community with your message, as you wish it to be told, may require that the college pay for the space or time. In other words, you may have to advertise.

Advertising may be the most effective method of communicating a complex story, one that could easily be misunderstood by an inexperienced reporter. Your best bet for explaining issues of tenure, accreditation, financing, or environmental impact may be to invest in airtime on radio and television or space in local newspapers.

The Media

The media, some argue, provide the means for building a sense of community out of a diverse collection of neighbors and neighborhoods. Indeed, responsibility for community building is a recently accepted role of the newspaper business. Because the media tell stories about different members of the community, they inform the community about itself. That information is the glue that holds the community together.

Although you may not feel comfortable with this community-building role, the media do play a key part informing the community about institutions important to it. That includes the community college. In theory, the media have no direct connection to the college. To them, it is just one more institution in a collection of institutions in which readers, listeners, and viewers have an interest. In general, the media want a story, one that will draw readers, listeners, or viewers to their particular publication, station, network, or Web site. A crisis provides the media with grist for their story mill. Almost any crisis that the media believe will interest their audiences will attract their attention, but particularly those that promise conflict and human interest.

A sexual harassment story promises both conflict and human interest. The harassed confronts the harasser. The harassed has been injured. Embezzlement promises conflict between the accused and the accuser, as well as human interest. Why would someone steal from a community college? Who was hurt by the theft?

To use the media to reach other audiences with important information, you must be prepared to be used by the media to tell a story. Knowing the nature of the symbiotic relationship helps you to plan what you will say to the media and who will say it. You probably want to take the "gotcha" out of the media's story, to soften any blow to the college and its personnel.

If you expect balanced reporting of a crisis at your institution, then you must be prepared to share information with reporters. You do not have to tell everything you know, but what you do tell must be the truth.

Members of the media are best reached by telephone, e-mail, and personal contact. Establishing and maintaining contact with selected reporters before a crisis hits will go a long way toward getting your story told with reasonable accuracy.

Know which audiences will be most important to you in any given crisis. Have a message platform from which to tell your story. Tell it using the most effective and efficient vehicle for reaching your key audiences.

7 Plans That Work

There are 1,160 community colleges in the United States, and their level of crisis preparation ranges from very thorough to not prepared at all. A survey of American Association of Community Colleges membership found a number of community colleges that not only had good crisis plans but were proud of the work that had gone into them and had found them extremely helpful in a time of stress and chaos.

There are references to some of those plans that have been tested in the real world elsewhere in this book. This chapter includes a look at two more community college crisis plans that could be a model for many others.

Broward Community College

Shortly after classes began for spring semester 2002, a young man walked onto the campus of Broward Community College, in Fort Lauderdale, Florida. He hesitated a moment, then spotted a girl making her way across the campus, books in hand, her smiling face turned toward the warm sun. Moving quickly but stealthily, he covered the distance between them, approaching her from the back.

Without a sound—no warning, no challenge, no cry—he pulled a gun and shot her in the back of the head. Nearby students, who had dropped to the ground or ducked at the sound of the shot, watched as she crumpled to the ground. The young man then stuck the gun in his mouth and pulled the trigger a second time.

The story of the murder-suicide, apparently the result of a quarrel between two people that had nothing to do with the community college, alerted the country to another "school shooting," this time at Broward.

Fortunately, the campus, under the leadership of President Willis Holcombe, was prepared. The four-campus, 60,000 student institution had revised its *Emergency Procedures Manual* in 2000.

Emergency Communications Preparation

Originally created to deal with hurricanes, the plan had to be modified because not all campus emergencies work on a hurricane's time schedule. Often there's no warning. A bookstore robbery in the early 1990s during which a manager was shot encouraged the modification. Each campus has its own emergency plan, but a collegewide communications plan overlays them all, forming a communications network.

The college has initiated but has not yet tried free e-mail for all students. The e-mail system was not activated in the recent shooting because students at other campuses were not immediately threatened. Shocked and saddened, yes, but they were in no danger from the event.

Students can consult counselors any time a crisis hits Broward, as those did who witnessed the double-shooting.

A phone tree provides the college president with a means of reaching campus administrators. An internal telephone system ties all four campuses together.

In the past, when the college used the e-mail system to contact students, it required that they access any messages. In other words, students had to know to look for a message. The new e-mail system will enable the college to send a message directly to every student.

President Holcombe expects the new e-mail system to be a "huge advantage to communicate with students." It will allow students to communicate directly with the president in times of emergency. The new system also allows him to send messages directly to the faculty. Faculty can then inform students in their classes of emergency situations as well as reach students wherever they can access their e-mail.

The college formerly used the telephone to notify students in cases of emergency but found that even a sophisticated telephone system can crash in a crisis. In the future, e-mail will be the primary way to reach students, with the telephone system as a backup.

The president of the community college serves as the primary spokesperson to internal and external audiences. The backup person is the public information officer. In Broward's case, that person is the director of college relations.

In the case of the murder-suicide shooting, the other campus leaders were notified using computer technology. President Holcombe can reach the provosts at the other campus via a listserv. Each campus can reach its own staff, passing the word through various methods along reporting lines: for example, provost to deans, deans to department heads, and so on. Each campus has mailboxes for faculty, employees, and students. Faculty use the system to post syllabuses, examination announcements, and other classroom materials. However, the system also can be used to communicate during, or about, emergencies.

The community college also maintains a Web site on which emergency information can be posted.

Lessons Learned

Dealing with the media during the recent crisis was different from dealing with the media following the bookstore shooting. Today, a college needs to be prepared for instant video coverage.

Within 15 minutes, MSNBC, CNN, and Fox were reporting live. Fox was videotaping from above the campus, showing the bodies before the emergency medical team had arrived. The news stations provided commentary as each showed the scene of the shooting. Their own commentary tried to relate the Broward shooting to similar events such as the Virginia law school murders and the Columbine massacre. The reporters developed their own "theories" about the connections between the Florida tragedy and others, trying to answer the question "What does this mean?"

In this, as in other incidents, President Holcombe felt it was important to be open to community agencies that could be helpful. He recommends that community college presidents get to know those agencies and incorporate them into the college's crisis management plans. For example, the superintendent of schools for the local public school district and the presidents of neighboring Florida Atlantic University and Florida International University coordinate decisions regarding the closing of schools because of weather or other threats to public safety.

The faculty and staff at Broward Community College were not ready for the police to investigate the shooting. One classroom building had to be closed because the police commandeered the first floor to interrogate witnesses. Trying to reschedule those classes into other buildings was a logistical nightmare, so classes normally held in that building were canceled.

Now, the multicampus Broward Community College is ready for emergencies. Each campus has its own emergency plan for dealing with crises, while the systemwide communications plan ties the several campuses together.

Indian River Community College

Indian River Community College (IRCC) serves more than 13,000 students along the Atlantic coast of Florida midway between Fort Lauderdale and the Kennedy Space Center. Five campuses are distributed among four counties: St. Lucie, Martin, Indian River, and Okeechobee.

Early one afternoon in the opening weeks of spring semester 2002, a female student was grabbed, pushed into a car, and driven away from the campus. She was subsequently raped by her abductor, a male former student, who had dropped out of the college. They had been lovers but were separated at the time of abduction.

Witnesses alerted campus authorities. Within minutes, the police were interviewing those who had witnessed the young woman's forced removal from the college. They got an accurate description of the abductor and of the car. By early evening, the abductor was in jail, and local social services personnel were helping the victim.

"Media merged on us," said David Anderson, vice president for student services and chief security officer. Anderson also serves IRCC as chief spokesperson during emergencies. He is from the area and has been with the college for 33 years, 25 of those in student services. The first contact came from the local newspaper by telephone to the campus public information office. This brief interview focused on the basic questions of who, what, why, when, where, and how. The reporter asked if Anderson could be interviewed. He, in turn, asked what the reporter wanted to know. The newspaper submitted a list of nine questions before a reporter arrived on campus the following day for the interview.

Even with this relatively controlled exchange, the "local media got it wrong," Anderson says. To one of the questions, "What changes would the community college make in its emergency response plan?" Anderson replied that the college would arrange to "debrief after the event and change procedures as necessary." The story headline claimed that the college would review its emergency plan and make changes.

As a general guideline, when speaking with the media as college spokesperson, Anderson is careful not to speculate. "I deal with what is," he says, not with what might be or might have been. Fortunately, he says, the "cameras did not come" to the campus. (IRCC is 36 miles from the nearest television station.)

In post-episode debriefing, the reviewing team found that the emergency plan worked well. Anderson estimated that it took just three to seven minutes from the time witnesses saw the abduction until the 911 call was connected. IRCC's president gave a very favorable appraisal of the community college's reaction to the event and the assistance given to the victim. The college's insurance consortium was likewise favorably impressed.

The young woman returned to her studies at IRCC. She received support from the college that included professional assistance from IRCC's counseling and wellness centers, as well as assistance from the county rape crisis center.

Emergency Communications Preparation

After 1999 Columbine High School shootings, and following a series of emergency incidents in Florida itself, a statewide conference was convened to take Florida's crisis planning beyond hurricane preparations. A prototype emergency plan was created that served as a model for Florida colleges. In response to the conference recommendations, IRCC expanded its crisis plan to incorporate law enforcement and emergency medical personnel from the four counties it serves. The college's modified prototype plan has been forwarded to the state, which is currently reviewing it. Pressure continues from the state government to create an emergency plan and to train the staff to use it.

Part of IRCC's modifications to its emergency plan began with an invitation to a local police SWAT team to look for potential danger spots on campus. Knowing it will seek assistance from local authorities in a crisis, IRCC keeps building schematics on computer disk in the student services office. Disks containing the schematics also are maintained in the offices of local law enforcement and emergency medical teams. The college's plan designates Anderson as the campus emergency response leader. As such, he takes his place in the command center alongside the law enforcement and emergency medical leaders when an emergency develops.

The emergency plan also calls for Anderson to meet and speak to the media. The college public information officer serves as his backup should one be needed. One of the objectives of the plan is to "insulate the president" from the media so he can focus on managing the crisis and the college. Anderson works with the public information officer on press releases and other statements issued to key stakeholders of the college.

Lessons Learned

Although IRCC has enjoyed fine relationships with personnel from the four counties, the recent abduction-rape reminded Anderson that local emergency officials can be extremely helpful. Law enforcement reacted quickly. Medical personnel and rape counselors responded with sensitivity.

The IRCC emergency plan worked, according to Anderson. It resulted in the arrest of the perpetrator and sympathetic, professional counseling for the victim and support for her as a student.

The college also may have learned the advantages of not being near a media center. The fact that cameras did not descend on the campus suggests the event was too far away for television crews to arrive in time to videotape relevant scenes. Not having the cameras on campus probably reduced the number of people aware of, and terrified by, the event.

8 When Someone Else's Crisis Becomes Yours

Sometimes, the challenges and aftershocks of someone else's crisis become your own as well. Your crisis plan needs to provide for this possibility.

Jefferson Community College is located in downtown Louisville, Kentucky, with a major elevated expressway running past the third-story windows of several classroom buildings. The college is a quarter-mile from a stretch of the expressway that is the scene of frequent multivehicle crashes. In fact, it has become known as "dead man's curve." Every day, trucks carry hazardous substances such as radioactive materials and explosive cargo on that eight-lane stretch of concrete and steel.

With dead man's curve in mind, Jefferson Community College has already drawn up an evacuation plan. The college administration is ready to manage a crisis that will be no fault of the institution and over which it will have no control.

The Borough of Manhattan Community College (BMCC) faced a similar challenge following the September 11, 2001, terrorist attack on the World Trade Center. Until September 11, BMCC lived in the shadow of the fourth-largest building in the world. After two hijacked jetliners slammed into the World Trade Center towers, the community college was thrust into the crisis simply because of where it was.

The main campus was three blocks away, but the newest BMCC building, Fiterman Hall, was immediately adjacent to World Trade Center Plaza.

The 15-story building contained 60 classrooms and scores of offices and had just reopened after a $65-million renovation.

Within 100 minutes after the terrorist attack, the two World Trade Center towers collapsed; later that afternoon, 7 World Trade Center, a 47-story office tower, also came down. As it fell, it nicked the top of Fiterman Hall, ripping away a corner of the building and piling debris up to the third floor on one side. The entire campus lost power, water, and telephone service. Fortunately, the building had been safely evacuated before 7 World Trade Center fell.

Two of the firefighters who perished rushing to rescue World Trade Center tenants were BMCC students. Four other students who were working in the doomed buildings died that morning. Another three staff members lost family members in the disaster.

And many students, faculty, and staff watched as bodies plunged from the upper floors of the trade center towers and then stared in disbelief as the towers themselves came down in a hailstorm of smoke, debris, and body parts. The emotional damage was deep and widespread, recalls BMCC president Antonio Perez.

To add to the college's problems, emergency response personnel, soldiers, and law enforcement officers began moving onto the BMCC campus, turning it into a command post and relief center.

Reflecting on that terrible day, President Perez recommends that when a community college facility is needed by organizations such as the police, firefighters, or other providers of emergency services, the college president should cooperate but never surrender control of the property. Perez stayed on campus around the clock the first few days; thereafter, other top administrators and campus security staff were always present. A few hours after the police and fire command post opened, a firefighter used an ax to break down a door because he wanted more office space. Perez made it clear to the fire department commander that he was willing to cooperate and that there were keys to unlock additional space. All they had to do was ask.

With the loss of telephone service, the college lost its e-mail capability; for a few days it was nearly impossible to communicate with students and faculty. Ultimately, President Perez took out newspaper advertisements to convey information to students about what was happening and when and how classes would resume.

By 11 p.m. on September 11, President Perez and his crisis team had begun the process of planning for the reopening of the college. They found a number of temporary-classroom trailers in Canada and arranged to lease them and have them moved to Manhattan. They hired contractors and developed a plan to create 40 temporary classrooms in the rented trailers and in existing space on campus. Crews worked around the clock, and classes resumed 19 days after the attack.

Although the focus of the crisis was the World Trade Center, BMCC was a victim and had to manage the crisis as if the college had been the terrorists' target. One of the lessons of September 11, President Perez said, is that a community college must be prepared to operate without computers. College administrators must have a plan for where they will meet to manage the crisis when they cannot work in their usual spaces. Computer data must be backed up off-site, and the plan should include a way to make payroll. He also noted that "cell phones are not a luxury." People may misuse them, but when the crisis hit, mobile phones saved a lot of time and energy.

BMCC had a plan that got the institution back on its feet and leadership that worked hard and set the example. If there had been no plan, the outcome would have been significantly different. But a disaster does not have to be as dramatic or close to home as the events of September 11 to cause serious trouble for your college.

On the heels of the World Trade Center and Pentagon attacks, an anthrax scare spread across the nation, and chemical and biological terrorism received new attention. Kathy Matlock, president of South Arkansas Community College, says there is nothing new about that concern on her campus.

"Although we are in an idyllic rural setting," President Matlock explains, "our community [El Dorado, Arkansas] has the unique distinction as one of the most dangerous places to live in the U.S. We are the site of many chemical and petroleum companies and have been conducting training for our community and region for years."

She says her college has special procedures in place for handling hazardous materials spills. "We have a procedure called 'shelter in place,' in which every building on our campus has an inside 'safe room' with emergency supplies." As a result of the planning and preparation at South Arkansas Community College, President Matlock says, the institution is a model in planning for an immediate response to hazards such as anthrax contamination.

Cataclysmic events with no immediate direct impact on your community college can so completely disrupt the routine activities of everyone on campus that you must make special efforts to ensure that the institution and its services continue as near to normal as possible, despite the confusion and unease triggered by the external event.

The attacks of September 11, like the shootings of presidents Reagan and Kennedy, affected the routine on college campuses throughout the United States, not just in the vicinity of the places where these events occurred. On a more local basis, political demonstrations or major sporting events can seriously affect traffic flow or otherwise divert the attention of students, faculty, and staff. The 1996 Olympics in Atlanta or the 2001 World Bank protests in Washington, D.C., are examples.

When this sort of disruption occurs, the media will want to know how the campus is responding, and students and staff will want to know not only what the college is doing to assist them in dealing with the disruption but how they should react.

In some cases, fallout from the disruptive event could go on for months, or even longer, but your crisis management plan only has to deal with the immediate actions that are recommended during the short period when the novelty of the situation makes everyone significantly less sure of what to do next.

Communications Priorities

If it is reasonable to say that the disruption is having no material effect on student and staff safety and productivity, and that your classes and services are being maintained at a normal level, then you should say it. If, on the other hand, the disruption has kept people from getting to classes or forced you to allow people to leave early to be with their families, then you should say that.

If an unpredicted external event is expected to be short lived, then it can reasonably be said that there will be a short-term disruption of classes and that you anticipate getting back to normal quickly.

When the story does not directly affect your college, or affects your college no more than its neighbors, then your institution should avoid becoming the center of journalists' attention. On one hand, you should not seek to become the story, unless unique circumstances force you to the forefront. On the other, if your college's institutional tenacity or heroics help your community "save the day," you should take credit in a modest way. (We provide an example of student heroics later in this chapter.)

If you communicate forthrightly with students and staff, they will be able to deal with their concerns in a way that will enable them to refocus on their studies and their work in short order.

If the situation requires that you invoke special security provisions, you must inform students, faculty, staff, contractors, and vendors. Government officials also need to hear from you.

Communications Messages

You will want to communicate that your community college is aware of the situation and has quickly taken the necessary steps to minimize the event's negative impact on students, faculty, and staff. You understand that this is not business as usual, but you are prepared for the unusual.

Remind the community that your college has a history of bouncing back when unusual circumstances hit. You are prepared to handle the present crisis wisely and safely and return to normal as quickly as possible. You are looking after the needs of students, faculty, and staff. Where possible and where appropriate, you are reaching out to your community to help it through this event. If the impact on your college and its students and staff is going to be long lasting or particularly widespread, you can offer stories that emphasize what is being done to lessen the disruption.

Communications with Students and Staff

Panic is always a risk when crisis strikes, whether it is your college's crisis or someone else's that affects you too. Planning and quick, accurate communications with students, faculty, and staff will eliminate or significantly reduce the chances of panic, says Chief Paul Sarantakos, director of public safety at Parkland College, a community college in Champaign, Illinois.

Recognize the Need to Reach Out

Within hours after the attacks on the World Trade Center and the Pentagon, people began reaching out to talk to loved ones. All kinds of people, including students who rarely called home, went home or called parents, siblings, or grandparents. They just needed to be reassured that some part of their world was still intact. The same thing happened after President Kennedy was assassinated and following the space shuttle *Challenger* explosion.

Administrators and faculty need to be ready to give students and employees the flexibility, time, and opportunity to make those reassuring contacts.

Students, faculty, and staff frequently need to be reassured that they are going to be okay, the college is secure, and campus life will return to normal as soon as possible.

Communicating with the Media

Your community college should avoid becoming the "poster child" for the story, especially if it is a negative story. But if there is a positive story to tell, you ought to try to break through the clutter of event coverage to get at least a small mention of your success. Small articles in the beginning cycles of news coverage of a major story lead to longer feature stories in the days and weeks that follow.

Normal press release distribution methods might be disrupted. Fax circuits at your college or at media locations may be out; normal news contacts may be overloaded.

Reporters who normally cover your institution closely might be shifted to event-related assignments and be less likely to check voice mail or otherwise stay in touch. Routine planning should include gathering mobile phone and pager numbers for key reporters. Media lists should include the main news desk number at each outlet in addition to reporters' direct numbers.

Advertising

Consider placing paid advertising thanking students, faculty, staff, and vendors for their assistance in getting past the event and its impact. If the impact is going to be long lasting or particularly widespread, advertising can help you emphasize what is being done to lessen the disruption on campus.

Good News out of Someone Else's Disaster

Oklahoma City Community College (OCCC) is six miles from the site in downtown Oklahoma City where a truck bomb exploded on an April morning in 1995.

OCCC president Robert Todd had just returned to his office after attending a prayer breakfast. The blast rattled glass walls in his office and windows all across campus. President Todd called campus security, but no one there knew the source or the location of the explosion. It was not long, however, before the Oklahoma City television stations began to show live pictures from the vicinity of the Alfred P. Murrah Federal Building.

Nursing students and students in an emergency medical technician training program began to mobilize almost immediately. After rounding up supplies and equipment, a contingent of OCCC students and faculty rushed to the scene and began working with other emergency responders. Some students stayed at the scene and helped search for victims for days.

The college had a positive story to tell but still had all the issues that go with a major disaster—fear, uncertainty, and emotional distress. Also, President Todd said that once he learned it was a government building that had been attacked, it occurred to him that his institution consisted of government buildings, so the college implemented stepped-up security.

Once Oklahoma City got past the first few weeks, OCCC began to review its crisis preparedness. President Todd said it became clear the institution had a pretty good plan for natural disasters, but the OCCC crisis plan was not adequate for terrorist attacks. It has since been improved to help guide the administration when, in his words, "you don't think too clearly."

He recommends that the college chief executive officer delegate the job of crisis team leader to someone else. In the case of OCCC, President Todd assigned that responsibility to the vice president for business and finance. He also says the college has developed checklists to go with each potential crisis in its plan so that the little details are not overlooked.

President Todd learned from his experience that it is not enough for the administration to communicate with students, staff, and the community. Speculation is not acceptable. "It must be credible communications," he stresses.

Anticipate as best you can, he further advises. Have the best plan you can put together, and make sure you have good people to implement it, but do not become consumed with worrying about crises. Above all, President Todd says, community colleges need to keep in mind that "our primary purpose is student success and helping students achieve their goals."

Eight Things to Consider When It Is Someone Else's Crisis

1. Keep in mind that while internal communications are always important, they are never more important than after a tragedy.

2. Reassure students and staff that the community college will continue operations and that their classes and jobs are not affected.

3. Be prepared. Even if your institution was not involved in any way, students and staff are more likely than ever to question everything, including their personal and job security and campus safety.

4. Remind students and staff of campus security procedures and take the opportunity to refresh everyone's familiarity with evacuation procedures.

5. Contact the Red Cross about sponsoring a blood drive at your facility.

6. Consider offering counseling at the campus or remind everyone of student and employee assistance programs that provide grief counseling.

7. If students or staff from your college are directly involved in the crisis, keep everyone on campus informed about their status.

8. Be sensitive. Individuals respond to disasters in different ways. Productivity will likely be affected. Be encouraging and give students and staff time to grieve. If staff notice that someone continues to seem distressed after two or three days, consider referring that person to a counselor.

9 Smoldering Crises Are the Biggest Threat

Smoldering crises are much more likely to occur on your campus than sudden crises or dramatic terrorist attacks. And it may be more difficult to identify the crisis potential in the early stages. That is because it is usually a problem that management fails to spot, avoids, ignores, or misunderstands in terms of its potential severity.

Human nature and campus political concerns often obscure the problem or its crisis potential, and problems like this sometimes go away on their own—which is what management hopes will happen. Some administrators are loathe to admit to themselves that there is trouble brewing because they believe such problems reflect on the quality and effectiveness of their leadership.

It does not help any that mismanagement and human error frequently strike the spark that starts the situation to smoldering.

Early Warning Approach to Crisis Management

Even better than successfully managing a smoldering crisis is keeping one from getting started in the first place.

A *management early warning system* is an information-gathering process. Administrators need to encourage faculty and staff to pay attention to what is happening around them and be aware of developing problems. The staff must also be convinced to tell someone in the administration if they suspect a crisis is possible. If your faculty and staff are reluctant to point out potential problems, this may be because they fear a "kill the messenger" reaction. If that is so, you have a smoldering crisis already.

Deans should encourage faculty in their departments to be alert and to encourage the staff in their offices to likewise be on the lookout for potential problems. If the staff call potential issues to the attention of the faculty and faculty members alert the deans to possible problems, then most smoldering crises can be resolved before they become public issues.

Some Basic Rules for Managing a Smoldering Crisis

Do Whatever Is Realistic to Prevent Public Disclosure

The objective is to resolve the problem and stop it from escalating into a public issue, but whatever you do must be legal, moral, and ethical. Recognizing that there is a potential problem is a big step toward solving the problem and preventing it from ever becoming a public crisis.

Anticipate the Reactions of the Affected Stakeholders

Anticipating how students, faculty, staff, and alumni will react to news of the smoldering crisis is useful in developing a plan to deal with it. If significant negative reaction will occur if the problem erupts into public view, then it is easier to make a successful case for resolving the problem before it ever gets out of hand. If the problem cannot be avoided, then anticipation of public reaction will help guide the crisis team in developing a strategy for managing the crisis and minimizing the damage.

The biggest difference between a sudden crisis and a smoldering crisis is the amount of time between learning of a crisis and responding to it. In a sudden crisis, the media may be outside the president's office before you know the problem even exists. In a smoldering situation, you may have hours, days, or even weeks between the time you learn of the growing trouble and the time it becomes public and you have to begin responding publicly.

Balance the Community College's Academic, Business, Legal, and Communications Priorities

As you develop a strategy for dealing with a smoldering crisis, consider its impact on all aspects of the management of your community college. You cannot always do that in a sudden crisis because there are too many decisions that have to be made quickly. But in a smoldering crisis, you will usually have time to consider the academic, business, legal, and communications issues and the relative impact of each decision you must make in each of those areas.

Make Sure Your Key Stakeholders Hear First

It is vital to future relations between the administration and all of your key stakeholders that they hear the bad news as well as the good news from you and not from the local newspaper, radio station, or television station. In a smoldering crisis, you will usually have time to make a good estimate of how and when the crisis will become public. Knowing when allows you to prepare messages and presentations for each of those key audiences, identify and prepare a spokesperson for each audience, and settle on a timetable, place, and method of informing them of what is happening before they hear about it from another source. For example, if you believe the story is going to break on the local 6 p.m. news, then notify your key audiences late in the afternoon before they hear about the bad news from the media, but too late for them to leak it or contribute negative reaction to the media.

Timing is critical. You cannot inform key audiences too early or the media may hear about your crisis from one of them before they hear about it from you. When setting your communications timetable, start with the time you expect to notify the media and then work backward. Community college representatives can be designated to meet with, call, fax, or e-mail specific audiences, all within an hour of any public announcements. There can be exceptions, but this is the general rule of thumb. It reduces the chance that one of those key stakeholders will contact a reporter and try to pre-empt or undermine your communication strategy.

The Less Said the Better, but Be Prepared to Respond to Inquiries

'No comment" is a red flag to reporters, and failing to take or return media calls is tantamount to saying "no comment."

The media are looking for a "gotcha!" If reporters can say they found out something, this implies that you were not forthcoming. But if you announce the problem and what you are doing to fix it before reporters finds out on their own, you have taken the "gotcha" out of the story. Reporters have been known to downplay stories that were revealed by the organization itself. The attitude is, "If the organization is willing to talk about the problem, then it must not be a big deal."

Work to Get News Media Coverage over with Quickly

Many problems can be limited to one-day stories if the administration responds effectively and quickly. For every day the story continues, its damage gets harder to undo. If you can get a satisfactory response or explanation into the first story, you may end up with a one-day story. If you cannot give reporters enough information for the first day's story, you guarantee yourself at least a second-day story, and for every day you fail to adequately answer the public's questions, you drive the story to another day.

Anticipate How Your Adversarial Stakeholders and Competitors Will Leverage the Problem

When you are identifying key audiences, take it one step further and determine which category each audience fits in—are they advocates, adversaries, or "ambivalents"? It is important to craft messages for each stakeholder group. You will present your position one way for audiences who are known to support you. You may not need to expend as much time and energy on adversaries if they are not likely to even consider becoming advocates. And when you address ambivalents, you must be careful not to say anything that will push them off the fence and into an adversary's camp.

And you do have competitors. Other educational institutions are competing for students and faculty, and many organizations are pursuing the same dollars you depend on to keep your community college functioning.

Assess How Well the Crisis Was Managed and What Worked

Just as with a sudden crisis, if it looks as if you are going to experience a smoldering crisis, you might as well learn from it. Review what worked and what did not. Find out who on the crisis team was effective and who was not. Then make the necessary adjustments so that you will be even better prepared the next time.

Managing a Smoldering Crisis Step by Step

Define the problem and its crisis potential and establish what you know for sure. What *don't* you know? What could be the disclosure scenario?

When will it become public? (This is *very* important.) How will it be revealed? Would the crisis be of interest to the news media?

You may have hours, days, or even weeks to answer these questions. But as with a sudden crisis, you cannot begin to make decisions and develop responses for your various audiences until you can confirm what happened (you must know for sure *what* happened), who was involved, when and where the crisis occurred, why it happened, and how it happened.

Step 1: Fact Finding

Some crisis plans include a questionnaire that guides the team through the fact-finding process:

- What facts do we know about the crisis at the present time?

- When did this first occur? How long has it been going on?

- Who is involved or implicated? What has been their role?

- What are the related political problems or other complications?

- Who else knows about the situation? What have the been doing about it?

- What is likely to be the next negative development? How soon will it occur?

- What is unknown? What is being done to find out?

- What are the sources of this information? How has it been verified?

The crisis team must anticipate the likely disclosure scenario that would make the crisis "public." If an administrator has been caught embezzling college funds and the authorities are notified, the most likely disclosure will occur when an indictment is filed or when an arrest warrant is served. You can ask the prosecuting attorney when the indictment will be unsealed or when an arrest warrant will be served and plan your response to coincide with that date.

You can assume the news media will be interested based on the nature of the smoldering situation and what the media have covered in the past.

Step 2: Focus on Reactions

Focus on the reactions of key stakeholders when they become aware of the smoldering crisis.

Anticipate stakeholders' reactions based on:

- their affinity for the institution
- how similar groups have reacted in the past when this kind of crisis has occurred

Define the advocates, adversaries, and ambivalents who are likely to become interested and get involved in this crisis.

- Note what will they want to know and their likely reactions.
- Project the impact (including the financial effects) of their reactions.
- Pinpoint stakeholders whose reactions will have the greatest impact if the crisis erupts.
- Try to predict how these stakeholders' top management will become involved.
- Estimate the amount of time and direct involvement of top administrators and the direct and indirect costs of their involvement.

Develop a management strategy for key stakeholders' likely reactions. These will vary depending on the nature of the disruption and how key stakeholders perceive it will affect them.

Step 3: Reaction Strategy

Concentrate on the stakeholders who can have the biggest influence and financial impact. Sometimes that will be alumni, other times faculty, and other times students, staff, or regulators.

Focus on the common concerns and reactions that will have to be addressed and develop strategies to minimize negative reactions.

Develop consistent themes and messages that can be conveyed with empathy. The key is to maintain the loyalty of your advocates, discourage your adversaries, and keep your ambivalents neutral. With that goal in mind, define the steps you will take to minimize negative reactions of advocates, adversaries, and ambivalents and build your communications plan around it.

Step 4: Sell the Plan

Estimate the management time and out-of-pocket expenses based on what has to be done and who is responsible for each action item. Use these time and cost estimates to brief management and determine if the problem can effectively be resolved before it becomes a crisis.

If you are unable to prevent the smoldering situation from becoming a full-blown public crisis, then you must establish a *trigger point* at which you will implement your reaction plan. If a college employee will be arrested for embezzlement tomorrow, you should plan to inform staff first thing in the morning and have a standby statement ready for media inquiries. You should also be ready to send a blast e-mail at midmorning to key alumni and other important supporters assuring them that procedures are in place to prevent this kind of loss again and that no education programs will suffer as a result of the theft.

The Bottom Line

Prevention is the best approach to the smoldering crisis. Know the vulnerabilities of your college. Keep an eye on the competition. Assess the human-interest potential of the crisis, should it find its way into the news. And be sure to maintain an operations and communications response plan.

If prevention does not work, then crisis control is the next best thing. Effective crisis control or crisis management requires that you coordinate legal, operations, and communications functions; "walk in the shoes" of the news media and your adversaries; think beyond the crisis itself; and understand that words are not enough—you must also act in ways that will make sense to your audiences, both internal and external.

Appendix A
Sample Document: Media Policies and Guidelines

MEDIA POLICIES AND GUIDELINES

Overview

[Your organization] recognizes that any crisis at one of its facilities will be of significant interest to the news media. The public has a right to be informed and has the duty to see that they get the facts on a timely basis, generally through the news media.

Our objective is to be as cooperative as possible in providing information on all aspects of the crisis, the impact it is having on our various constituencies, and the condition of those who may have been affected, as long as the information will not interfere with the emergency response activities, the well-being of our constituencies, and the concerns of their families.

I.   General Policies

To be as fair as possible to all members of the media, the following policies must be adhered to:

1.   All announcements, updates, and answers to questions will be provided by a designated spokesperson at the site of the crisis or at a specified [your organization] Media Information Center. Any information relating to the crisis which is obtained at other locations or from

other sources may not be accurate and could necessitate a correction.

2.   Press releases, photographs, and videotapes will be distributed only at the Information Center.

3.   The schedule for briefings, during which questions will be answered, will be based on the status of the crisis and the availability of an authorized spokesperson to provide updated information.

4.   Information on the crisis will be limited to confirmed facts and a general summary relating to progress since the last briefing. Minor changes will not necessarily be reported if the crisis response personnel consider them to be a normal part of the recovery progress. Significant changes will be reported as soon as the officials at the scene have confirmed the data and assessed the effects on the crisis.

5.   Reports summarizing the medical condition of any students, staff, or faculty affected by the crisis will be the responsibility of the medical team at the hospitals where they have been admitted and will be provided by an authorized spokesperson at that facility. Elaboration on progress reports will only be provided by an authorized medical spokesperson.

II. Media Briefings

1.   All briefings will be scheduled in advance, with the times based on the priorities of the crisis team and authorized spokespersons. Thirty-minutes notice will be provided when the crisis is still in a critical phase. A briefing schedule for the following day will be posted when the situation has stabilized.

2.   Comments made by designated spokespersons during the briefing, as well as the answers to questions, will be recorded and transcribed. All information provided during the briefing will be "on the record."

3.   TV cameras must be positioned at the rear of the room where briefings are being conducted. No cameras will

be allowed directly in front of the podium if they block the view of seated journalists.

4. Movement of TV cameras during briefing will be limited to the aisles along the sides of the room. TV cameras will not be allowed on the podium when briefings are in progress.

5. No TV or radio microphones should be allowed on the podium if ample mult-box connections are provided for radio and video feeds directly to broadcast equipment.

III. Interviews

1. All interviews with [your organization] officials involved in the crisis must be scheduled in advance through the communications staff on duty in the Information Center or through [your organization] public relations.

2. In most instances a minimum of 18 hours will be required to schedule interviews. The only exception will be if major news developments have occurred. In those instances, the scheduling of interviews will be determined by [your organization] media personnel, based on the availability and preferences of appropriate spokespersons.

3. A member of the [your organization] staff will be present at any individual interview. The interview will be recorded and transcribed to provide written documentation of what was said.

4. All information will be "on the record," and there will be no "unidentified sources" for information relating to the crisis. Any source of information is to be identified by name to ensure that the information can be verified if there is a question about its accuracy.

5. Rumors and/or speculation will undoubtedly occur during the crisis. [your organization] policy is not to respond to this information until the facts can be checked. If information is not provided by a designated [your organization] spokesperson, or is not disclosed

during a scheduled interview or briefing of the media, it will not be considered verified.

IV. Photographs and Videotape

1. To minimize disruption during a time of great stress, [your organization] reserves the right to provide the photography/videotaping at the site of a crisis during the initial hours, using photographers and TV camerapersons hired by [your organization] specifically for this assignment. The results of their work will be made available to the news media in the Information Center.

2. If and when news media photographers and TV camera personnel can be allowed into the scene of the crisis, a designated representative will advise the news media of the restrictions that may have to be placed on their presence at the scene. They will be accompanied by [your organization] representatives and may be asked to leave the scene if they violate the restrictions that were established in advance.

3. In some instances, a pool arrangement may be set up to provide initial media coverage at the scene. [your organization] will specify the number and types of journalists who can be physically accommodated at the scene and the time they will be allowed to complete their work. The news organizations covering the crisis will determine the pool composition based on those specifications and how the visual and written coverage will be distributed to other news organizations. If there may be any physical danger to the journalists in the pool while they are at the scene, they will be required to sign a "Hold Harmless" agreement before being allowed to participate.

4. A variety of black and white photographs, color slides, videotapes and other graphic materials may be made available at the Information Center to provide visual support for the news media's coverage. Contact the communications representative on duty to review and select from these visual materials.

V. Authorized Spokespersons

1. A chief spokesperson may be designated for the crisis, based on its nature and location. _____, _____or _____ or their designee, will serve as the primary spokesperson on an ongoing basis throughout the crisis.

2. Responses to media inquiries also may be provided by other [your organization] staff and outside experts who may serve as designated spokespersons for the organization and are identified by name in the resulting news material.

VI. Disclosure of Information

1. During the initial phase of the crisis, all news will be released simultaneously at the site (if one exists) and at the [your organization] Information Center to ensure timely, consistent distribution of information to the media.

2. No news will be disclosed at the site that is not provided at the Information Center. In some instances, as with media briefings or interviews, disclosures will occur at the [your organization] Information Center that will not be made known immediately at the site.

VII. The [Your Organization] Information Center

1. The Information Center will be open on a round-the-clock basis if it appears that the crisis will not be resolved in the first 24 hours. Hours will be adjusted from that point on depending on the situation.

2. [Your organization] will have a media relations representative, who is a designated spokesperson, on duty whenever the Information Center is open. The representative, whose name will be posted, will be responsible for responding to media questions, arranging interviews, obtaining photographic/video material, and assisting with other media needs.

Media Briefing Tips for Spokespersons

1. **Pause Before You Answer**—Give yourself plenty of time to consider the question and its implications. If you can, think of a way to explain your answer in a visual way that will be understood by television viewers. Reporters are not in a hurry, and if they are, that is unimportant. This is your interview, so take your time in responding to their questions.

2. **Keep Your Answers Short**—Two or three sentences at most. Answer the question in the first sentence, explain it in the second and third sentences and that is all. The more you say the more you are likely to regret saying it.

3. **Do Not Speculate**—It is human nature to try to talk your way out of something you are not sure of, especially if you are nervous—and you will be. If you do not know the answer, the most intelligent response you can give the media is something along the lines of "I'm not absolutely sure. Let me check into that and get back to you."

4. **If the Question Is Tough, Pause and Think**—You may know the answer but feel uncomfortable in responding because you are not sure what you want to say or how. That is the time to pause. Silence is the reporter's problem, not yours. Take a few seconds to think your answer through. It may seem like an eternity, but it usually only takes a moment to get your thoughts organized.

5. **Close Every Question with a Pleasant Look**—A quiet smile, where it's appropriate, gives the reporters—and the public—the impression that you are sure of what you are saying. Another advantage of the smile is that it will be the last thing the TV viewers will see when the tape is edited in the newsroom.

6. **Think of the Reporter as a Means to an End**—They are concerned, they are interested, and they really want to know what is happening so they can tell the folks back home. You may not like the reporter or the media in general, but they are the only ones who can help the

public to grasp what you want them to know about what has happened. So be patient and tell them in common sense terms that anyone can understand and appreciate.

7. **Emphasize and Re-Emphasize the Most Important Points**—It is perfectly all right to repeat yourself, especially if these are the most important ideas you want to convey. You need to communicate those ideas in as many ways as possible because you are never going to be sure what statements or quotes a reporter will use. Take every opportunity to make the important points over and over again, using terms to which everyone can relate.

8. **Show Compassion**—In your remarks, remember to communicate your concerns for those people directly affected by the situation (that is, students, staff, faculty, family members, friends, or others) and that "we're doing everything possible to help them through this difficult time."

9. **Stay on the Record**—You have no idea what the reporter will use, so do not give him/her an indication there may be more to the story than you want to disclose. Going off the record is dangerous because any good reporter will verify that information with other people and pursue that angle, leaving you with no control of the information he or she is obtaining. The key is to know the limits of what you will talk about and stick to them.

10. **The Interview Is Not Over When the Interview Is Over**—Off-the-cuff remarks are a natural tendency after the last question has been asked, but they may well wind up in the story. Remember that the interview is still going on until the reporter is physically gone or has hung up the phone.

11. **Record What You Are Saying**—There is no law against it, and the reporter is likely to be doing the same thing, especially in telephone interviews. Tell him/her you are recording the conversation so you can review it and learn from the experience. What you also are doing is keeping the reporter honest and increasing the likelihood your statements will be used accurately and in context.

Appendix B
Sample Document: Debriefing and Evaluation Questions

COMMUNITY COLLEGE CRISIS DEBRIEFING AND EVALUATION QUESTIONS

The questions that follow provide a basis for debriefing and evaluating the organization's response to a crisis. They are general in nature to stimulate discussion among the debriefing participants. More specific questions should grow out of responses to these general questions.

The debriefing can include reconstructing the incident timeline and guiding participants through a process to make sure they each understand the sequence of events and their impact upon employees and the organization as a whole, as well as people and agencies outside the organization. Evaluation judges the effectiveness and efficiency of the organization's response.

The questions focus on evaluation.

1. In what ways, if at all, could the crisis have been avoided or reduced in magnitude?

2. What worked well during the initial crisis response? What did not? What caused problems, surprises, and/or disappointments?

3. What little things made a difference in our response? What little things might have made a difference if they had been available?

4. In what ways, if at all, could we have saved money in our response to this crisis?

5. How well did our existing operations and communication plans work?

6. What needs to be changed to make them more effective?

7. What is our assessment of the news media coverage and the impact of the coverage on the organization? Students? Faculty? Staff? Management? Alumni? Supporters? Reputation? In what ways, if at all, could we have managed media coverage more effectively?

8. Who in our organization really stood out—positively and negatively—in terms of their contribution, or lack of it, to the crisis response? In what ways should these people be recognized and rewarded? Retrained or replaced?

9. What would we do differently if we had it to do all over again?

Resources

Articles

...Crisis management as part of emergency response planning. *Environmental Manager*, Jan 1995, v6n6, p7-8.

Abstract: Regardless of the kind of emergency for which response plans are made, being prepared for an operational response is not enough to assure that the company is truly and fully prepared. Creating a cohesive plan to respond to outside forces and then following it should an accident occur can help assure that a range of potential legal and stakeholder relations liabilities are minimized.

...How the postal service plans to stop 'going postal'. *Government Executive*, Dec 1996, v28n12, p14.

Abstract: The U.S. Postal Service's workplace violence prevention program, the most comprehensive of its kind in government, includes zero tolerance for workplace threats; a crisis management plan; violent incident drills; and threat assessment teams to identify workplace risks and recommend abatement plans. A video in production, "Separation Without Violence: A Peaceful Parting," teaches humane ways of firing employees.

Anderson, Pat. Telling it like it is. *Marketing Week*, Apr 22, 1994, v17n7, p63-67.

Abstract: Those involved in protecting the good name of countries, organizations, and individuals say good crisis management helps their clients to twist fate and exploit a potential disaster as a prime opportunity for some free prime-time promotion. Kleshna Handel of Handel Communications says that one of the greatest crimes in a crisis is to be an ostrich and pretend it did not happen. Only one thing is worse, she says: saying something that shows a company does not care. Crisis management specialist Mike Regester concurs that openness is an essential part of any crisis management campaign. Another essential part of crisis management is preparation, either for a crisis for which a company is responsible or for somebody else's.

Aspery, John and Woodhouse, Norman. Strategies for survival.
Management Services, Nov 1992, v36n11, p14-16.

Abstract: The future of a business depends on how the crisis that may be just around the corner is managed. A business is most likely to manage a crisis successfully if it has prepared for the worst possible scenario. A sensible starting point is to identify and analyze areas of risk. A crisis manual must include key contacts, prepared contingency statements, and draft news releases. Crisis management means crucial decision-making under pressure. The golden rule is to react—but not overreact—immediately. Press inquiries should be seen as opportunities, not problems. The radio or television interview by the nominated spokesperson will influence the way the business is perceived. Other essential audiences should not be neglected.

Augustine, Norman R. Managing the crisis you tried to prevent.
Harvard Business Review, Nov/Dec 1995, v73n6, p147-158.

Abstract: Almost every crisis contains within itself the seeds of success as well as the roots of failure. Finding, cultivating, and harvesting that potential success is the essence of crisis management. And the essence of crisis mismanagement is the propensity to take a bad situation and make it worse. The six stages of crisis management are: 1. avoiding the crisis, 2. preparing to manage the crisis, 3. recognizing the crisis, 4. containing the crisis, 5. resolving the crisis, and 6. profiting from the crisis.

Barton, Laurence. Crisis management: Selecting communications strategy.
Management Decision, 1990, v28n6, p5-8.

Abstract: Crisis management experts agree that preparation is the key to successful crisis communications. However, in a Western Union survey of 2,000

U.S. companies, only 57 percent of those surveyed have planned for crisis communications. Fink (1986) argues that some companies ignore warning signs that spell danger. A regularly updated crisis plan can be the best source of defense for managers. This plan can outline procedures for contacting key employees during holidays and weekends, restoring facilities and services, cooperating with local and state regulatory agencies, and reconstructing damaged facilities. Effective relations with the news media are one of the most crucial areas of crisis management. According to Jay Jaffe, president of Jaffe Associates, effective media relations begin by telling the company's story quickly, openly, and honestly.

Bernstein, Jonathan. The 10 steps of crisis management. *Security Management*, Mar 1990, v34n3, p75-76.
Abstract: There is no such thing as a business without crises, and proactive preparation costs less than postevent reaction. Preparation can be divided into 10 basic steps: 1. Identify a crisis management team. 2. Identify spokespersons. 3. Train these spokespersons. 4. Establish communication protocols. 5. Identify the important audiences. 6. Anticipate crises, which will identify preventable situations and thus allow for preparation of appropriate responses. 7. Assess the situation by ensuring that the crisis management team receives all incoming information. 8. Identify key messages. 9. Decide on communication methods after the available options are evaluated by a professional. 10. Prepare for dissatisfaction with the plan.

Bland, Michael. Training managers to handle a crisis. *Industrial & Commercial Training*, 1995, v27n2, p28-31.
Abstract: The best way to prepare an organization for a crisis is to start with the training and work backwards to development of a manual, because crisis management calls for an instinctive understanding of the psychologies involved and a high degree of flexibility. A typical development program to prepare an organization for a major crisis is outlined. A description is presented of how to sell such a course to a management already committed to first preparing a plan and the author's approach as a trainer.

Cheney, Karen. Managing a crisis. *Restaurants & Institutions*, Jun 1, 1993, v103n13, p51-66.
Abstract: The most effective way to approach crisis management is to always

assume a "pre-crisis" mode. Because the first round of media coverage determines whether a restaurant is a victim or villain, it is important to have a Crisis Response Team with a communications crisis plan to handle the situation. Any response team should be small enough to allow members to make decisions quickly, but large enough to include key personnel. One crucial member is the designated spokesperson—the only one who should make public statements. This will help avoid the release of contradictory information. The team should hold periodic sessions to anticipate every possible problem. Besides dealing with the media, restaurants must communicate with their employees—the people with firsthand contact with customers.

Chenier, Errol. The workplace: A battleground for violence. *Public Personnel Management*, Winter 1998, v27n4, p557-568.
Abstract: The workplace has become a battleground for violence in society. With so much violence in newspapers, on television, and in homes, the workplace is not immune to this crisis. Employers will have to plan strategies and implement programs that will protect employees from rising violence on the job. Policies and procedures, crisis management teams, security, and Employee Assistance Programs will have to be in place if incidents should occur.

Cobb, Robin. Pushed on to the public stage. *Marketing*, Nov. 6, 1997, p16-18.
Abstract: While most organizations recognize the benefits of gaining the awareness of the public generally—and of their customers, investors, or legislators specifically—few equip their management and technical people to handle this. Yet their in-house press officers or public relations consultants can only take the message so far. A few executives are media naturals, but the vast majority can benefit from tuition. Each of the following areas is discussed: 1. types of training, 2. what you learn, 3. what it will cost, 4. the role of public relations professionals, and 5. crisis management.

Cohn, Robin J. Pre-crisis management. *Executive Excellence*, Oct 1991, v8n10, p19.
Abstract: A company that assumes a crisis will happen will survive the impact if it does. Pre-crisis management develops a crisis management plan long before a crisis ever occurs. One way to help handle a crisis before it occurs is to develop positive relationships with key publics and the media to

generate support during crucial times. The crisis management plan should be focused on five principles: 1. corporate responsibility, 2. public support, 3. leadership, 4. communication, and 5. employer support. In order to have significance, the five principles must be endorsed by top management.

Crandall, William. How to choreograph a crisis. *Security Management.*, Apr 1997, v41n4, p40-43.

Abstract: To evaluate its response capabilities in an emergency, Concord College in Athens, West Virginia, formed a crisis management team in December 1995. The team met over the next several months to construct a crisis management plan that could protect the 2,400 students and about 200 faculty and staff who might be on the school's campus when an event occurred. By the spring of 1996, the team had a final plan and agreed to test it by staging a drill. The overview of the drill plan, its execution, and follow-up evaluation provide a model for any security manager looking to test an organization's crisis management plan.

Cullen, David. When winging it won't work. *Fleet Owner*, May 1996, v91n5, p108.

Abstract: At the recent Interstate Truckload Carriers Conference, Janine Reid of the Janine Reid Group discussed how advance planning is the key to crisis management, especially when dealing with the news media. According to Reid, whatever the root cause of the crisis, certain techniques for handling media attention work equally well—as long as a company is prepared to use them. Reid's techniques for dealing with the press included: tell the truth, use understandable language, condense information, and make sure that information is accurate.

Dilenschneider, Robert L. Work place crises aren't what they used to be. *Communication World*, Oct/Nov, 1997, p24-27.

Abstract: Workplace crises in a global economy are changing from the traditional problems of oil spills, labor disputes, product recalls, and environmental disasters to those involving people. Sexual harassment, discrimination, workplace violence, sabotage, theft, insider trading, and fraud are more likely to happen in organizations in all parts of the globe. The author urges public relations professionals to be proactive in advising management to prevent these new crises.

Fitzpatrick, Kathy R. Ten guidelines for reducing legal risks in crisis management. *Public Relations Quarterly*, Summer 1995, v40n2, p33-38.

Abstract: The challenge of the Crisis Manager is to balance public relations and legal considerations and determine where the organization's greatest exposure lies. Guidelines for reducing legal risks are: 1. View legal counsel as a resource. 2. Analyze legal and other trends. 3. Learn from others' mistakes. 4. Be prepared to manage the public disclosure of compliance information. 5. Respond to marketplace rumors. 6. Avoid litigation through communication. 7. Anticipate litigation in the development of company documents. 8. Choose spokespersons trained in both law and public relations. 9. Work with legal counsel to institute a compliance program. 10. Promote ethical behavior within the organization.

Gonzalez-Herrero, Alfonso and Pratt, Cornelius B. How to manage a crisis before—or whenever—it hits. *Public Relations Quarterly*, Spring 1995, v40n1, p25-29.

Abstract: Even though corporations are more vulnerable to crises than they were in the past, a majority of them are reluctant to adopt integrated crisis-management plans. Ways that organizations can respond effectively to human-provoked, organizationally induced crises are discussed, and a model crisis management process is described. The model focuses on two corporate examples: McDonald's hot coffee spill and Intel's Pentium flaw. An analysis of these crises suggests some correspondence with the biological model in which an organism passes sequentially through phases of birth, growth, maturity, and decline. The crisis life cycle can be used to foresee expected outcomes for each stage of the cycle. Under timely management intervention, however, a crisis might not reach its growth and maturity stages. The crisis management process is characterized by four main steps: 1. issues management, 2. planning-prevention, 3. the crisis, and 4. the post-crisis.

Greenberg, Keith Elliot. Experts offer tips on how to deal with the unthinkable. *Public Relations Journal,* Dec 1993, v49n12, p6, 8.

Abstract: The bombing of the World Trade Center in New York City in early 1993 forced public relations practitioners like Mark Marchese of the Port Authority of New York and New Jersey to deal with terrorism. In the months following the attack, Marchese implemented an ongoing public relations strategy that others will probably duplicate as terrorism becomes a greater threat in the United States. Marchese says the explosion confirmed the wisdom of taking precautions in the event of a terrorist attack. Thomas Preston of Preston Group says terrorism is not confined to acts perpetrated in the name of some international crusade. Social terrorists regularly cause disruption in protest of abortion, animal testing, and timber industry practices. Robert Irvine of the Institute for Crisis Management (Louisville, Kentucky) says that from a public relations standpoint, terrorism differs from other crises in that it is not a victim organization's fault: The public will support the victim. When an act of terrorism does occur, it is best for public relations people to tie in with the, Federal Bureau of Investigation (FBI) and local police. Their public information officers have much experience with the media in crises.

Hall, John R. In the jaws of a crisis. *Directors & Boards*, Summer 1991, v15n4, p17-20.
Abstract: Change, turmoil, and crisis are likely to dominate the United States in the years ahead. If organizations are to survive, they must learn to deal effectively with change and crisis, not as a matter of necessity but as a matter of choice. Crisis management has evolved from a public relations issue to one of professional status. Good Crisis Managers utilize four key tools: 1. the crisis audit, 2. the crisis team, 3. practice, and 4. the crisis center. Ashland Oil Inc. learned from experience what items are needed for crisis management when an oil spill on January 2, 1988, threatened the water supply of suburban Pittsburgh, Pennsylvania. As a result of this crisis, Ashland developed the following crisis management "recipe": 1. Go to the site promptly. 2. Obtain first-hand information. 3. Marshal all available resources and equipment to clean up the mess. 4. Contact political officials. 5. Offer restitution. 6. Call in third parties (experts). 7. Meet the press. 8. Establish a local office. 9. Stay on the job. 10. Become personally involved.

Hickman, Jennifer R. and Crandall, William. Before disaster hits: A multifaceted approach to crisis management. *Business Horizons*, Mar/Apr 1997, v40n2, p75-79.
Abstract: Crisis management is a developing area that seeks to ease the impact of events such as natural disasters. Important as a disaster plan is, its effectiveness can be enhanced if a multifaceted approach is used. Information systems, human resources, public information, and operations

must all take on various crisis mode functions until the disaster has passed. The three critical functions of top management in planning for and managing a disaster are: 1. assembling the crisis management team, 2. developing worst-case scenarios, and 3. creating a crisis management plan. Backing up all computer files on a regular basis is a must for any organization. Crisis management should address the psychological assistance employees might require. A designated member of the crisis management team should be chosen to communicate with the media and handle all public relations situations that may arise. The most crucial goal in operations management is to secure and protect the plant and equipment in the best manner possible.

Kamer, Larry. Crisis planning's most important implement: The drill. *Communication World*, Dec/Jan 1997-98, p27-30.

Abstract: Practice is the third ingredient in crisis readiness along with plans and preparation. Suggestions for testing the crisis plan and drilling employees in the use of the plan are made.

Kauffman, James. A successful failure: NASA's crisis communications regarding Apollo 13. *Public Relations Review*, 2001, v27n4, p437-448.

Abstract: In April 1970, NASA faced its second major crisis when an explosion on board Apollo 13 threatened the lives of its three astronauts. NASA's handling of the crisis not only would determine the fate of the three astronauts, but also the image of the space agency and possibly the future of American manned space exploration. This article examines NASA's crisis communications regarding Apollo 13. It argues that NASA and the Nixon administration's handling of the crisis not only bolstered NASA's image, but it also may have helped to gain crucial public and congressional support for continued manned space exploration. The space agency succeeded by responding quickly to the crisis and communicating honestly and openly with key publics. The study demonstrates how a successful response to a crisis can enhance the image of an organization.

Lurie, Geoffrey D. and Ahearn, Joseph M. Ten rules for successful crisis management. *Leadership & Organization Development Journal*, 1991, v12n2, pi-iii.

Abstract: An informal management style, called Theory R for "Radical," includes 10 rules for successful crisis management: 1. Make certain that the real crisis is identified. 2. Remember that power is what managers have and what the opposition thinks the manager has. 3. Do not become involved in areas where the personnel are inexperienced. 4. Go outside the opposition's experience and get the opposition on your "home field." 5. Make the opposition play by its own rules. 6. Do not let issues drag on too long. 7. Keep the pressure on and keep in mind that a good crisis manager does not let up or declare victory at the first sign of success. 8. Remember that the threat is usually more terrifying than the problem itself. 9. Keep in mind that there is nothing to lose and everything to gain—but it is important make sure there is truly nothing to lose. 10. Remember that the price of a successful attack is a constructive alternative.

Mallozzi, Cos. Facing the danger zone in crisis communications. *Risk Management*, Jan 1994, v41n1, p34-42.
Abstract: Every company, large or small, should have a crisis communications plan in place that outlines general policies and procedures so that it can adroitly handle emergencies, accidents, and the resulting public relations issues. If there is one key lesson crisis management experts have learned over the years, it is that facts alone do not win arguments; perceptions do. Consequently, any company facing a crisis must take into account the public's perception of the event and the company's response. Determining what constitutes a correct response is never easy.

Martinelli, Kathleen A. and Briggs, William. Integrating public relations and legal responses during a crisis: The case of Odwalla, Inc. *Public Relations Review*, Winter 1998, v24n4, p443-460.
Abstract: The crisis management communication strategies employed by Odwalla Inc. during its juice contamination crisis are examined. An analysis of the content of published responses made by the Odwalla officials showed that public relations response strategies dominated legal response strategies throughout the crisis, followed by mixed public relations and legal strategies. This case provides a clear example of the collaborative approach to crisis management in terms of legal versus public relations strategies. In addition, Odwalla exerted control over the crisis through its recall, the development of a process to eliminate the problem, and raising the issue of pasteurization.

Mathews, Wilma K. "No comment" is never the right comment. *The Public Relations Strategist*, Fall 2001, v7n4, p31,33.

Abstract: Find other ways to avoid providing information: "I can't give you any information on that because..." While your explanation may become the quote or sound bite, it reveals a willingness to cooperate *when* you have the information which is better than saying nothing.

Maynard, Roberta. Handling a crisis effectively. *Nation's Business*, Dec 1993, v81n12, p54-55.

Abstract: In the current age of heightened consumer awareness and rapid news dissemination, preparing to manage crises and respond under fire can help mitigate the effects of almost every kind of problem, ranging from allegations of defective products to workplace accidents. According to Hal Warner of Manning, Selvage, and Lee, when crises are prepared for, decisions made during a crisis will be more rational and better received, and the crisis will be of shorter duration. To prepare a crisis plan, key employees should be consulted about what could happen, however unlikely. A spokesperson should be designated. If a situation calls for talking with the news media, this should be done without delay. A basic tenet of crisis management is that a company must demonstrate that it cares, particularly if there are injuries or deaths, regardless of whether the company contributed to the accident.

Moskovitz, Mike. Thurston High School shooting tragedy: The media downpour. *Public Relations Tactics*, Jan 1999, v6no1, p20-22.

Abstract: The media management plan when a 15-year-old opened fire in a high school cafeteria, killing two and wounding many others involved six main steps: 1. assemble a crisis team, 2. quickly analyze, but do not overanalyze the situation, 3. set up a media information center, 4. communicate as quickly as possible, 5. provide steady communications on the status of the crisis, and 6. make the media a partner, not an enemy.

O'Donnell, Jayne. Damage control. *Working Woman*, Apr 1999, v24n4, p83-84.

Abstract: During a public relations emergency, always remember that the first thing said travels the farthest, says Dick Starmann, former McDonald's senior vice president, responsible for crisis management worldwide. Honesty is the best policy, but so is heeding good legal counsel: What you say can end up being used against you. Of course, the best way to manage a crisis is to prevent one from occurring in the first place. Look at areas where your company is most vulnerable. Experts also recommend getting to know the reporters on your company's beat.

Patterson, Bill. Crises impact on reputation management. *Public Relations Journal*, Nov 1993, v49n11, p47, 48.

Abstract: Businesses and other organizations will always face critical situations. Thus, the effort to control negative situations continues to become more sophisticated. While crisis management is a plan of action to be implemented quickly once a negative situation occurs, reputation management is a strategy that is used all year, utilizing a proactive approach. Crisis management is evolving into reputation management for a number of reasons. First, reputation management should attract more attention from top management. Second, more organizations are facing situations that have real potential for harming their reputations. The most important rule in defending, preserving, or enhancing a reputation is that public relations practitioners work at it all year long, regardless of whether a crisis strikes.

Richardson, Bill. Why we need to teach crisis management and to use case studies to do it. *Management Education & Development*, Summer 1993, v24n2, p138-148.

Abstract: To meet the growing challenge of our crisis-prone world, managers in those organizations that create and have to deal with crises need to learn to minimize the likelihood of adverse effects or to mitigate them. Some general attributes required of crisis managers are: 1. awareness and proactivity, 2. knowledge of and familiarity with helpful concepts, 3. left- and right-brained thinking capability, 4. empathic, communicative, and group decision-making qualities, 5. ethical confidence, and 6. emotional strength. Case studies can help managers make better decisions on the crisis phenomenon. They help to increase awareness of the crisis problem and contribute to the theory base from which managers can draw.

Spaeth, Merrie. Lawyers: An additional danger in a crisis. *Public Relations Tactics*, Oct 1999, v6n10, p10-12.

Abstract: Warning: Lawyers are trying to enter the public relations profession in the area of crisis management. Gives tips on how to protect yourself from this travesty. Lawyers should not try to manage crises because they rebut charges and quibble with facts, deny charges, want information before responding, and are poor writers. Protect yourself from lawyers taking over by preparing with team management.

Stein, M. L. Training lawyers to deal with the media. *Editor & Publisher*, Oct 26, 1991, v124n43, p14-15.
Abstract: Tom Mira, president of Mira Communications, a communications training, public relations, and crisis management firm, advises lawyers on how to deal with the media. Mira says that it is the nature of the law business to attract controversy, and it has become more prevalent because U.S. society has become so litigious. Mira coaches attorneys and executives to follow several rules in media encounters: 1. Have a clear message and objective to communicate. 2. Keep it brief and simple. 3. Try to establish rapport with the reporter. 4. Since many reporters are expert at reading upside down, clean the desk before an interview. 5. Never say anything to the press that should not be printed or repeated, no matter what off-the-record assurances are given. 6. Do not get angry.

Thomas, Kimberly. Remembering April 20: The Columbine tragedy from a PR perspective. *Public Relations Tactics*, July 1999, v6n7, p1+.
Abstract: The community outreach officer for West Metro Fire Protection District in Littleton, Colorado, discusses the immediate events surrounding the announcement of the shootings at Columbine High School. To be able to deal effectively in such situations, she suggests networking in advance, anticipating possible scenarios, keeping monitors on phones, monitoring pages, and scheduling interviews, and taking control of news conferences that get out of control.

Walter, Kate. Are your employees on the brink? *HRMagazine*, Jun 1997, v42n6, p57-63.
Abstract: According to the 1996 survey on workplace violence conducted by the Society for Human Resource Management, work-related aggression is on the rise. Managers need to understand what types of behavior are inappropriate and where they can turn for help to resolve problems. Types of high-risk employees and their behaviors are discussed. Systems recommended by

Crisis Management International for reporting and recording incidents include: 1. a policy statement on workplace violence, 2. a notification system, 3. a threat response team, and 4. training for front-line employees. The Center for Aggression Management offers a two-day training program designed primarily for front-line supervisors.

Weide, Sonny and Abbott, Gayle E. Murder at work: Managing the crisis. *Employment Relations Today*, Summer 1994, v21n2, p139-151.

Abstract: Workplace homicide incidents are occurring at a rate of more than one a week across the United States. In the event of a workplace homicide, the crisis management effort must be truly accomplished to avoid long-term problems within the organization. The course of action in response to a crisis is somewhat guided by the circumstances of each event, but there is a common path to follow: 1. Engage counseling. 2. Assemble a crisis management team. 3. Call the victims' families. 4. Prepare a media statement. 5. Clean up the work site. 6. Set up employee information meetings. 7. Meet with the managers. 8. Initiate internal and external investigations. 9. Establish an employee response committee. 10. Set up an employee reentry support program. 11. Handle insurance/workers' compensation claims. 12. Set goals in the future to focus efforts.

Books

Babbage, Keen J. 911; *The School Administrator's Guide to Crisis Management*. Lancaster, PA: Technomic Publishing Company, Aug. 1996.

Barton, Laurence. *Crisis in Organizations: Managing in the Heat of Chaos*. Cincinnati, OH: South-Western Publishing Co., 1993.

Bolz, Frank; Dudonis, Kenneth J.; Schulz, David P. *The Counter-Terrorism Handbook: Tactics, Procedures and Techniques*. Boca Raton, FL: CRC Press, 1996.

Burak, Patricia. *Crisis Management in a Cross-Cultural Setting*. Washington, D.C.: NAFSA, Association of International Educators, 1995.

Caponigro, Jeffrey R. *The Crisis Counselor: The Executive's Guide to Avoiding, Managing and Thriving on Crises that Occur in All Businesses.* Southfield, MI: Barker Business Books, Inc., 1998.

Davis, Lanny J. *Truth to Tell: Tell It Early, Tell It All, Tell It Yourself: Notes from My White House Education.* New York: The Free Press, 1999.

Dougherty, Devon. *Crisis Communications: What Every Executive Needs to Know.* New York: Walker & Company, 1992.

Grove, Andrew S. *Only the Paranoid Survive! How to Exploit the Crisis Points that Challenge Every Company & Career.* New York: Doubleday, 1999.

Hurst, David K. *Crisis & Renewal: Meeting the Challenge of Organizational Change.* Boston, MA: Harvard Business School Publishing, 1995.

Irvine, Robert B. *When You are the Headline: Managing a Major News Story.* Louisville, KY: Harmony House Publishers, 1987.

Johnson, Kendall. *School Crisis Management: A Team Training Guide.* San Bernardino, CA: Borgo Press, 1992.

Lerbinger, Otto. *The Crisis Manager: Facing Risk & Responsibility.* Mahwah, NJ: Lawrence Erlbaum, 1997.

Lichtenstein, Robert. *How to Prepare for & Respond to a Crisis.* Alexandria, VA: Association for Supervision & Curriculum Development, 1995.

McCarthy, Shaun P. *The Function of Intelligence in Crisis Management.* Brookfield, VT: Ashgate Publishing Company, 1997.

McLoughlin, Barry. *Risks & Crisis Communications: Pocket Tips Booklet.* Washington, DC: McLoughlin MultiMedia Publishing, Limited, 1998.

Millar, Dan P. and Smith, Larry L. *Crisis Management and Communication: How To Gain and Maintain Control.* San Francisco, CA: IABC, 1998.

NOVA (Young) Staff. *Responding to Communities in Crisis: The Training Manual of the Crisis Response Team.* Dubuque, IA: Kendall/Hunt Publishing Company, 1996.

Ogrizek, Michel; Guillery, Jean-Michel. *Communicating in Crisis: A Theoretical and Practical Guide to Crisis Management.* New York: Aldine DeGruyter, 1999.

Opalewski, Dave. *Crises Response Planning: A Procedure Manual for Schools.* Kalamazoo, MI: Balance Group Publishers, LLC, March 1998.

Petersen, Suni. *School Crisis Survival Guide: Management Techniques & Materials for Counselors & Administrators.* Paramus, NJ: Center for Applied Research in Education, 1991.

Regester, Michael; Larkin, Judy. *Risk Issues and Crisis Management.* London: Kogan Page Ltd., 1997.

Sandoval, Jonathan. *Preparing for Crises in the Schools: Manual for Building School Crisis Response Teams.* Brandon, VT: Clinical Psychology Publishing Company.

Sikich, Geary W. *It Can't Happen Here: All Hazards Crisis Management Planning.* Tulsa, OK: PennWell Books, 1993.

Stevenson, Robert G., ed. *What Will We Do? Preparing a School Community to Cope with Crises.* Amityville, NY: Baywood Publishing, 1998.

Traverso, Debra Koontz. *The Small Business Owner's Guide to a Good Night's Sleep: Preventing and Solving Chronic and Costly Problems.* Princeton, NJ: Bloomberg Press, 2001.

Walters, Lynne M.; Wilkins, Lee; Walters, Tim. *Bad Tidings: Communication and Catastrophe.* Hillsdale, NJ: Lawrence Erlbaum, 1989.

Wright, Martyn. *Managing Competitive Crisis: Strategic Choice & the Reform of Workrules.* New York: Cambridge University Press, 1999.

Young, Davis. *Building Your Company's Good Name: How to Create and Project the Reputation Your Organization Wants and Deserves.* New York: AMACOM, 1996.

Index

About the Authors

Larry L. Smith is a graduate of Indiana University's journalism and radio-TV departments with a degree in education. He began his journalism career as a news photographer, working for United Press International and later as a reporter and editor for a series of Indiana newspapers.

Smith then moved to radio, where he worked as a reporter, anchor, telephone talk host, and radio news director. He then switched to television, working as a political reporter, anchor, and later as news director of stations in Fort Wayne and South Bend, Indiana, and Louisville, Kentucky. He took a hiatus from journalism to serve as press secretary to Dan Quayle, then representing Indiana in the U.S. Senate.

In 1994, Smith joined the Institute for Crisis Management (ICM), based in Louisville. He was named president early in 1999 and acquired the company in December of that year.

With ICM senior consultant Dr. Dan P. Millar, Smith cowrote an updated edition of *Crisis Management and Communication: How to Gain and Maintain Control*, published by the International Association of Business Communicators. He was also a contributing editor to *Crisis Communications in Healthcare: A Delicate Balance*, published by Washington Business Information, Inc. He has also taught at Indiana University Southeast as an adjunct professor in radio and television news, and broadcast news writing.

Dan P. Millar joined the staff of ICM in the mid-1990s. He has been a professor of communication and a business consultant for more than 25 years.

Millar chaired the Department of Communication at Indiana State University for nine years. He received the Kaleb Mills Distinguished Teacher Award at Indiana State in 1999. He taught at Central Michigan University (where he also received teaching awards), Bowling Green State University, Michigan State University, and Port Huron Junior College before coming to Indiana State.

Millar has served as vice president of the Central States Communication Association, vice president of the Hoosier chapter of the Public Relations Society of America, and vice chair of the Public Relations Division of the Speech Communication Association. His most recent research focuses on the aftermath of crises and the methods organizations use to re-establish normalcy and a sense of community. Millar has published more than 25 articles and four books.